Danni's
JUKE JOINT
COMFORT FOOD

Danni's
JUKE JOINT
COMFORT FOOD

Modern-Day Recipes, Ole Skool Flavas

Danni Rose

HARVEST
An Imprint of WILLIAM MORROW

HarperCollins books may be purchased
for educational, business, or sales
promotional use. For information, please
email the Special Markets Department at
SPsales@harpercollins.com.

FIRST EDITION

Designed by Melissa Lotfy

Photography copyright © 2023 by John
Hanney

Concrete, lights, and wood backgrounds
and neon arrows © Shutterstock

Library of Congress Cataloging-in-
Publication Data has been applied for.

ISBN 978-0-06-328105-9

23 24 25 26 27 TC 10 9 8 7 6 5 4 3 2 1

In memory—

I dedicate this book to the memory of my father, Haywood Roseborough, the man that always had a cup in his hands. I know he's up there in heaven with my uncles and brother, and Johnnie Taylor also is up there, singin' the blues and arguing about whose angel wings are the most fly. And let me tell ya, hunny, with them around, I'm sure Jesus is still turnin' water into wine.

CONTENTS

ACKNOWLEDGMENTS

Now, y'all know I have to thank some folks!

God, you are my everything, and I am forever grateful that you chose little ole me to be a vessel to the world. Without you, nothing is possible, but with you by my side, I know that ALL things are possible. Everything I have is because of you. And I'll add more to that before I ever take it back!

My daughter, Riley, I dedicate this book to you: you have inspired me to love, dream, and thrive without limits, and I pray that as you watch me navigate my journey it will allow you to do the same.

Mama Z, Veda, Haywood Jr., and my crazy-ass family: thank you for always having my back. Your support means the world to me, and I will always be grateful!

To my wonderful team: Brandi Bowles, hunny, thank you for having my back and thinking of me. You are one of a kind and a true gem to the world.

Stephanie Fletcher, hunny, thank you for your patience, advice, guidance, and listening ear, and thank you to the wonderful team at Harvest for your hard work! What a ride this has been, but I wouldn't change a thing. I appreciate all of you for allowing me the space to create and be myself without change, and I will cherish you and this experience forever!

I am extremely thankful for my wonderful supporters. Your unwavering support means the world to me; I do not take it for granted, and I can't thank you enough, from the bottom of my big ole southern heart.

INTRODUCTION
What's a Juke Joint?

I get asked all the time what a juke joint is. That doesn't surprise me: juke joints, sometimes affectionately referred to as "holes-in-the-wall" or "shot houses," are not really well known, and they're really not supposed to be—they were created to be hidden gems on purpose. This is a side of Black history—going back to the era of Jim Crow laws—that isn't often talked about, but it's a side that you should really get to know! The juke joint experience is incredible, if I do say so myself. Now, let's be real: we all know that secret places, honeycomb hideouts, plus bad choices make the best stories!

Because back then, Black people in the South weren't allowed into white establishments, so we did what we always do *best*, and that is CREATE our own vibe! Juke joints were invented by our community to do one simple thing: give folks a place to have good food and a good ole time.

You see, people would go then—and still do—to their local hole-in-the-wall to dance, laugh, talk smack, and drink a bunch of good-ass DRANKS after a long day . . . chile, just like you do now after work, for girls' night, or when life is getting on your damn nerves. Except nowadays, people choose fancy restaurants serving weaker-than-water DRINKS and underseasoned appetizers. I'd rather put on some casual clothes and step into a hole-in-the-wall. Juke joints are usually found along the southern delta beltline of the Deep South. It's the type of place that if you know, you know. You could have a juke joint right in your neighborhood and not even know.

See, in a juke joint, people just wanna have a good time and leave their worries at the door. All the other things in life don't matter when you step inside. It's the most welcoming environment you will ever experience. I can get a couple strong dranks and a fried fish or chicken plate for less than twenty dollars and have the time of my life, too? Chile! Sign me up every time!

I was so blessed to know those happy times from a young age, being as I grew up in a juke joint. My father owned one, called Haywood's Place, on the west side of Birmingham, Alabama, right next door to our house. Now, he wasn't the only one in our neighborhood who owned one, but his juke joint was the most lit, considering the crazy stuff I saw growing up. Hunny, my mama taught Sunday school, and my daddy owned a liquor house (another name for juke joints), so it shouldn't surprise you that I love whiskey and communion! I can pray for you or cuss you out—it's up to you. I dance to the beat of yo' music, as my daddy would say!

Lemme walk you through Haywood's Place, so you can picture being in a juke joint yourself. Imagine a little wooden house where the smell of fried food and cigarette smoke fills the air and smacks you right in the face as soon as you step in. The symphonious sounds of Bobby Womack, Betty Wright, or Johnnie Taylor fill the room. Assorted tables and chairs are scattered around the room, and barstools lined up along the bar. My father had a jukebox that sat to the left and a dance floor as shiny as a new penny to go with it.

The ladies there smell all sweet, like White Diamond perfume, and the men have gold rings on every finger and toothpicks hanging out of the sides of their mouths. It's loud, not because of the music but because of the people and all their activities. Folks

Above: A typical weekend at Handsome Brutes Club in my hometown

Left: My "quiet storm" brother, Haywood Jr., me, and my nephew Justin

Below: My dad, mom, brother, and uncles hanging out at Haywood's Place before heading to a Bobby Womack concert

are talking smack 'cuz they're drunk, dancing and shouting about "get down now" or laughing, telling jokes, catchin' up, and gossiping. You can just about get any drink made with simple stuff—a Sex on the Beach, Jack 'n' Coke, gin and juice, ANYTHING with Hennessy, or whiskey neat. Let's not forget that everything is usually garnished with those bright-red maraschino cherries (which are such a waste in my opinion, but who am I to talk!). Oh! And best of all: you can also get the best fried fish sandwich, pork chop sandwich, or fried chicken wings you've ever had! Now, at my daddy's place, my mama did most of the cookin' in the back. Don't get me wrong, my daddy could burn with the best of them, but, hunny, it was NOTHIING like my mama's fried fish and chicken. I guess everything is just betta with a feminine touch. The food and dranks are always served in a paper product or in plastic cups, with plastic utensils, just laid back and easy.

Of course there is always a bottle of hot sauce at the bar because hot sauce is like a good stiff drank—it makes everything better! Just ask the barkeep and they'll hand it to ya!

Even if you've never been to a juke joint, you might recognize that enterprising mentality, which is all around us today in other parts of our lives. Juke joints were created because Black people did not have a space in white establishments to have a good time, to thrive, and to be themselves. When I got started creating on social media, I didn't see a space for people that looked like me, I didn't see a space for people that sounded like me, and I didn't see a space for people that dressed like me and talked like me to just be their authentic selves. Creatives are making their own movies, they're financing their own dreams, and they're not waiting for the traditional circles to accept them. Everyone can live a juke joint lifestyle in their own way. You can create a space for yourself and people who are likeminded to feel safe, you can break down barriers, and you don't have to take no shit! You can create wonderful memories while creating wonderful things.

I grew up in a neighborhood that wasn't the best, but we sure had the best times, and it all started at Haywood's Place—seeing my sister and her college girlfriends sneak into the juke joint to drink strawberry daiquiris,

my father throw men out for being assholes, and my mama and her friends sit around at club meetings eating chicken salad and gossiping about the mess in the church. In this book I'm paying tribute to those good times and the juke joint lifestyle, the neighborhood, and the family recipes I loved so much growing up. Although we didn't have a lot of money, we for sure didn't let that stop us from having a ton of fun. My mama always say you ain't gotta have a lot of money to make the best of times. And that's exactly what we did.

All the wonderful hood memories contributed to make me the woman I am today and inspired the recipes you'll find in this book.

This is the way I like to make the foods that I enjoy. Some are traditional. Some are

things I'd put on the menu at my own juke joint—call it "Danni's Place." Hey, you have to speak it into existence, right?! Until then, I am so happy and so blessed to share with you things that are truly dear to my heart. We're making some delicious and nostalgic food, and it's all just down-right SOPPED UP! Some things you might be able to relate to, and some things I'll introduce you to, like my favorite burger spots in Birmingham that my father used to take me to. Either way, we are gonna laugh, dance, and smack our mouths, and I'm taking a page from my crazy daddy's playbook, and that is to say what's on my mind. These recipes are so endearing to me, and I hope that you love them just as much as my friends and family do. Turn up your favorite ole skool playlist, pour a li'l drank or wine in a plastic cup, and make whateva dish makes you say, "I want *that* right there." Trust me, you can't go wrong. All my food is easy to make and tastes incredible! Hunny, don't let me take up too much time talking here . . . . **Let's get to the good part—turn yo' music up and turn the page!**

RED CUP COCKTAILS

COCKTAILS

a.k.a. Dranks 'n' Drinks

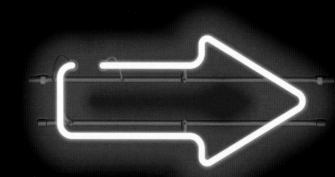

There is a difference between a drink and a drank, chile.

And depending on what's happening in your life, you will need *both* at different times.

Lemme explain the difference. A *drink* is like a glass of wine or a mild little cocktail. Like a tequila sunrise, or a mimosa. A *drank* is what you have at the juke joint, family gatherings, or someone's house at the Friday night fish fry, and it's always served outta a red plastic cup. When I am trying to be a bougie LA suburban mom or am having a dinner meeting, I have a *drink*. If it's the weekend, or I'm near some type of blue water, or hell, if I just need to clear my mind because, you know, "life," that's when I'm gonna have a few DRANKS!

Growing up in the South, you start drinking coffee and beer as a baby. Something about "it kills the worms," or at least that's the lie they told us . . . So anyway, right or wrong, we all took a sip of your mama's wine cooler or daddy's Bud Light before we could even walk! You already know that if alcohol is involved, we are about to have a blast laughing or spend the evening breaking up our uncles' fights. Regardless, we would do the silliest thangs. But I always say, "Bad choices make good stories," and you know I ain't lyin'! Anyway, drink responsibly, my friends. Cheers!

JACK & PEPSI SLUSHIES
a.k.a. "Don't Drop the Drank"

Startin' where it all started . . . my daddy's juke joint. We're taking Daddy's favorite, Jack and Pepsi, and mixin' it up slushy-style. I like adding vanilla to this, like the vanilla cola drink I loved as a little girl.

One of my favorite stories about my father is from when we were all at my sister's for a barbecue. He was outside grillin' and sippin' and talkin' smack with my brothers. Some kinda way, he backed up and slipped and fell backward, but he never dropped his drank and didn't spill one drop as he lay flat on his back in the yard! Hunny, that body dropped, but that Jack Daniel's didn't! To this day, we all laugh about it, and I've named this drank in honor of him.

Top these with a big ole cherry, or squeeze in a little fresh lime juice for a bit of a mouth pop at the end!

MAKES 2 COCKTAILS

4 ounces (½ cup) whiskey, preferably Jack Daniel's

One 12-ounce can (1½ cups) Pepsi

2 ounces (¼ cup) Simple Syrup (page 211)

1 teaspoon pure vanilla extract (optional but really good!)*

2 lime wedges or maraschino cherries

I. Pour the whiskey, Pepsi, simple syrup, and vanilla (if using) in a blender with 2 cups of ice and blend until smooth.

2. Divide between two highball glasses.

3. Garnish each glass with a fresh lime wedge or a cherry.

---

* Now listen, if you're gonna use that cheap vanilla extract or imitation, hunny, you may need 2 teaspoons instead. Start with 1 teaspoon and then add more if you want.

Juke Joint
SPIKED TEA

My aunt Debra would make this tea every year at the family reunion—it was one of the best nonalcoholic things I've ever drunk. Growing up, Auntie Debra would always say to us, "Bad choices," if she caught us doing things we weren't supposed to do, like adding Hennessy to this tea behind her back! I was able to steal her recipe, and yes, I spiked it! So, sorry, Auntie Debra, we about to make some reeeaaal bad choices with this one.

PS—If you wanna do it Auntie Debra's way, keep it virgin and don't add any liquor. Not only is it real good on its own, but also by addin' the liquor to each glass (instead of to the pitcher), the kids can enjoy some, too.

MAKES 1 PITCHER, 4 TO 6 SERVINGS

2 cups lemon-flavored powdered tea mix (I like Lipton)

1 cup sugar or Simple Syrup (page 211)

One 12-ounce can (1½ cups) lemon-lime soda, such as Sprite

½ cup lemon juice, either fresh (about 6 juicy lemons) or bottled

4 to 6 ounces (½ to ¾ cup) liquor (optional; brown liquor works great with this, whether whiskey, dark rum, or Hennessy)

Lemon wheels

1. Put the powdered tea and sugar in a large pitcher and fill halfway with water. Stir well to dissolve the tea mix and sugar.

2. Add the soda and lemon juice, stirring well to mix. Taste and adjust the flavas—you can add a little more tea mix, sugar, or soda if you want.

3. Fill each glass about halfway with ice, add a 1-ounce shot (about 2 tablespoons) of whiskey, fill with tea, and stir. Garnish with a lemon wheel and sip away!

Sparkling
JUKE JOINT SANGRIA

When you think about sangria, you think about fresh fruit and fresh flavors mixed with a little wine and alcohol. And to me that ain't nothin' but a spiked fruit punch bowl, something that we grew up on in the church. For things like women's day refreshments or a funeral, they always had a fruit punch bowl with fresh fruit in it to make it look pretty. I feel like that's the Black version of a sangria (only without the alcohol).

Now, I haven't been to Spain yet, but it's definitely on my bucket list. So I decided to make my version of a juke joint sangria, and it's filled with fresh fruit, juices, whiskey, and some other amazing delicious things. But this recipe is really all about what you are feeling! If you like white wine, use that! I suggest that you chill all your liquor before you make this.

MAKES 1 PITCHER, 4 TO 6 SERVINGS

1 apple (any kind), cored and cut into pieces
1 orange, cut into slices
2½ cups Grand Marnier

2 cups apple or pineapple juice
One 750 ml bottle sweet red wine, such as Roscato or another red blend

A few shots whiskey or cognac
1 small bottle Prosecco, for topping

I. Put the fruit in a large pitcher, then add 1½ cups of the Grand Marnier. Allow the fruit to soak in the liquor for about an hour or so. (Be careful: the fruit will sneak up on you after you eat it!)

2. Once the fruit has soaked, add the juice, red wine, the remaining 1 cup Grand Marnier, and however much of your favorite whiskey or cognac you think will make you happy . . . Just let the spirit lead you.

3. Mix everything together, taste, and adjust.

4. To serve, pour into a glass with ice and top with a little Prosecco.

Fancy
CHURCH LADY COCKTAIL

When I was a little girl, the church ladies would serve refreshments after an evening service. Most of the time there'd be chicken or tuna salad, Ritz crackers, and fruit trays from the grocery store. Sometimes they'd serve a punch called Frampe (I do not know why it was called that), which was nothing more than lime sherbet in a big punch bowl with lemon-lime soda poured on top. Or they'd make a Kool-Aid punch with pineapple juice. BOTH were really great, but the red punch was my fave! And because I once saw a deaconess drinking out of a flask in the church parking lot, I thought it was only fitting to spike this red punch, too. Shhhhh, don't tell nobody, and if they ask what you're drinking, just tell 'em happy juice! This punch is perfect for large gatherings and parties.

MAKES ABOUT 1 GALLON

2 cups red powdered Kool-Aid, such as Tropical Punch or Cherry

2 cups sugar (yes, we're adding sugar to the Kool-Aid)

About 2 to 4 quarts (8 to 16 cups) hot water (you may not use all of it)

2 cups pineapple juice, or more if you want

About 2 cups rum of your choice

I. Grab a large pitcher that holds at least a gallon. Add the Kool-Aid and sugar and fill the pitcher about halfway with hot water. (I use hot water to help the sugar dissolve, and it makes the Kool-Aid all syrupy, but cold water is also fine.) Mix together.

2. Stir in the pineapple juice. Taste and adjust the flavas to your liking.

3. Once the Kool-Aid part is good to go, add in the liquor! Mix well and serve over ice.

BAMA BUSHWHACKER

Yes, we love our frozen drinks in the South! They are always a hit—easy to make and a really great way to hide the alcohol. Plus, in the South it gets hot as a ho in church, so it's always nice to have a frozen drink to cool down.

This drink tastes just like a frozen hot chocolate. It's slightly creamy and silky and goes down smooooooth. A pretty famous restaurant in Birmingham called Saw's BBQ makes a version that's considered a staple. Let's just say, too many of these will make you walk up to a stranger who's minding their business and ask them, for no reason at all, "What are you looking at?!" Can't say I didn't warn ya.

MAKES 1 OR 2 COCKTAILS

½ of a 15-ounce can coconut
   cream*
2 shots Kahlúa
1 shot vanilla vodka

1 shot rum
3 tablespoons chocolate syrup,
   or more if you want, plus more
   for the glass

Whipped cream, for serving
   (optional)

I.   Fill a blender halfway with ice, add the cream of coconut, Kahlúa, vodka, rum, and chocolate syrup and blend until smooth and creamy. If you want a thicker texture, just add a little more ice. Taste and adjust the flavor to your liking.

2.   Add a little more chocolate syrup to a glass or plastic cup and pour the drink. Top with whipped cream if you want.

---

*If you don't like coconut, you can substitute half-and-half or vanilla coffee cream; reduce the amount to ½ cup. I will say, you can't taste the coconut in this recipe at all; it just gives it a nice creamy sweetness.

Hennessy Peach
WINE COOLER SLUSHIES

When I was growin' up, my mama and her friends would always drink wine coolers to be fancy. (I guess it was the hood version of a white wine spritzer.) The coolers were sweet and delicious, and the ladies would add ice to theirs and shake 'em around to get 'em nice and cold.

Chile, you could hardly taste the liquor . . . and those are the dranks that sneak up on ya and get you lit! So be sure to take small sips of this one! Cheers to drinkin' fancy wine coolers.

MAKES 2 COCKTAILS

1 cup frozen peaches
1 shot peach schnapps
1 shot tequila

1 or 2 shots Hennessy (If you wanna add tequila only, you can. But if you wanna have fun, add the Henny!)
3 tablespoons agave syrup

2 tablespoons fresh lime juice (from 3 large limes) or bottled
White Zinfandel or your favorite white or rosé wine, for topping

I. Put the peaches and about 4 cups of ice cubes into a blender. Add the schnapps, tequila, Hennessy (if using), agave syrup, and lime juice.

2. Blend on high until everything is nice and frosty. You don't want it too stiff; if it's too thick, just add another shot of any of the liquid ingredients to loosen it up and blend again. If it's not thick enough, add more ice.

3. Pour it up and top it off with wine to taste!

SUBURBAN MOM

Since I live in LA now, my girlfriends and I have developed a suburban lifestyle, and we make no apologies for it, especially me, having lived in the hood the majority of my life. That said, one day my girlfriends and I went to a Mexican restaurant while our kids were at school, just like the Housewives would do. This place served sangria in their margaritas instead of tequila, and they were *muy bueno*!

In my version, I've added tequila *and* sangria, and this has become my favorite drank to make. It's even better when your kids are gone during the day! So let's make a batch or two of these and hope we can make it to car pool!

MAKES 2 COCKTAILS

6 ounces (¾ cup) fresh lime juice (from about 8 large limes)

4 ounces (½ cup) tequila (I like reposado)

2 tablespoons agave syrup or Simple Syrup (page 211)

1 ounce (2 tablespoons) Grand Marnier or triple sec

Salt or sugar, for the glass (optional)

4 to 8 ounces (½ to 1 cup) store-bought sangria of your choice

I. Put the lime juice, tequila, agave syrup, Grand Marnier, and 4 cups of ice in a blender and blend until smooth.

2. Give it a taste and adjust the flavas, if needed. You can also add more ice to thicken it.

3. Now, I don't like salt or sugar around the rim, but if you do, feel free to salt or sugar yours. (Wet the rim of the glasses and press into either sugar or salt to stick.)

4. Add about a shot (1 to 2 ounces, or 2 to 3 tablespoons) of the sangria to each glass and then pour the frozen margarita on top.

5. Finish each cocktail with another shot of sangria. And, hunny, try not to drink too many; we don't need you at the school cussing out the principal in your underwear!

COCKTAIL GRAPES

Oh, hunny! Boozy, chilled, and sugary, these cocktail grapes are just a bunch of sopped-up yumminess in every bite. You can enjoy them anytime, any way, or any day of the week . . . Snackin' on drunken grapes sounds like a good-ass vibe to me!

(Shhhhh—don't tell anybody . . . a boyfriend introduced these to me way back when. Let's just say, we ended the night in a really adventurous way.)

MAKES 4 TO 5 CUPS, DEPENDING ON THE SIZE OF THE GRAPES

2 pounds green seedless grapes, stems removed, washed well

1 bottle Champagne or sparkling wine

4 ounces (½ cup) flavored white liquor of choice, such as rum or vodka

1 cup sugar

I. Place the grapes in a large bowl and pour in the Champagne and liquor. Cover tightly and refrigerate for at least 6 hours, but overnight is best.

2. Drain the grapes in a strainer set over a bowl to save the liquid. (This liquid is good for making cocktails—just add juice!)

3. Place the sugar in a baking dish and then add the grapes, rolling them around so the sugar sticks while they're still wet.

4. Refrigerate and serve cold.

Juke Joint MIMOSAS

Most mimosas are made with a bunch of fruit juice and a little Champagne . . . but not this time. This is the way I like to make mine, and I know you'll enjoy it, too. It has three ingredients, and two of them ain't juice! For brunch I'd pair these with Cheddar & Scallion Pancakes with BBQ Pulled Pork (page 23). And be sure to sip this one slowly!

MAKES 4 TO 6 DRINKS

One 750 ml bottle really good
   Champagne

1 shot Grand Mariner per drink

1 tablespoon orange juice per
   drink

I. Grab your favorite glass, or if you're like me and prefer your drank in a red cup or plastic cup, use that.

2. Fill the cup halfway with Champagne, then top with Grand Marnier and juice.

BLUE MOTHER

The name says it all . . . This is strong! Proceed with caution, hunny!

MAKES 2 COCKTAILS

2 ounces (¼ cup) blue curaçao (see Tip)

1 ounce (2 tablespoons) gin

1 ounce (2 tablespoons) white rum

2 ounces (¼ cup) triple sec

1 ounce (2 tablespoons) vodka

6 ounces (¾ cup) sweet and sour mix

2 maraschino cherries

I. Put the blue curaçao, gin, rum, triple sec, vodka, sweet and sour mix, and 4 cups of ice in a blender and blend until smooth.

2. Garnish each glass with a cherry.

> **Tip** Blue curaçao has a low enough alcohol content to freeze. That means you can freeze it up in ice cube trays overnight. Then use those instead of—or with—the regular ice for a more powerful cocktail, a.k.a. rocket fuel.

THERE'S BREAKFAST

and Then There's Brunch

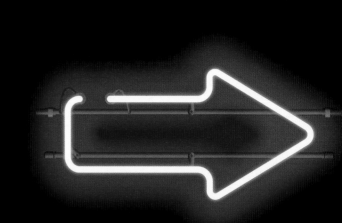

When you need a li'l somethin' somethin' in the morning . . .

whether that be somethin' to soak up that liquor from last night or just a li'l time to pamper yourself, these dishes are as comforting as a church lady's hug.

And I don't know about you, but going to brunch on the weekends feels so extra and luxurious to me. It gives "rich auntie vibes"—you know everybody has that ONE person in the family that thinks they are above everyone else! Bein' an adult these days includes a ton of responsibilities, so brunch is my new outlet. (My friends and I prefer day drinking and eating anyway!) I love to throw on a cute outfit and find the best spots to grab mimosas or a crisp, refreshing glass of St-Germain and Champagne, sitting on a rooftop deck, enjoying the sun. And if you find the right place, it can turn into an awesome day party, too. Talk about a good time . . . what's understood ain't ever gotta be explained, and I can make it home in time for a gooood nap! That's what I call being responsible.

So, this section is for all of my grown folks who wanna turn up a bit but still got thangs to do the next day. These days, folks are really tapping into preparing brunch-inspired dishes at home on the weekends, and I am here for it! These recipes are perfect for any time of day but taste even better on a sunny weekend morning. Invite a few friends over, or not. Make a couple Juke Joint Mimosas (page 17), drink way too many, and cook up some deliciousness.

CHEDDAR & SCALLION PANCAKES
with BBQ Pulled Pork

I'm gonna say straight up: I hate chicken and waffles. People think it's a southern thing, but if it were, then why ain't Waffle House sellin' it? I would rather sit in the front row at a Baptist revival drinking a glass of Hennessy than eat soggy-ass fried chicken all glopped up in a sticky, sweet sauce that's supposed to be on breakfast waffles. Enough about that. I've got a dish here that's gonna make you forget all about 'em!

This is why we eatin' a pile of tender roast pork with a tangy-sweet whiskey BBQ sauce and savory pancakes instead. But maybe chicken and waffles is your thang? Hey, I'm a cussin' Christian, so the last thing I'm gonna do is judge you.

I like my butta-milk, so you know I'm gonna grab that box of buttermilk pancake mix. And, hunny, you know me, I'm gonna put even more buttermilk in there. Why? Because I don't trust it, that's why! If your pancake batter is too thick after mixing it all together, then add a little more buttermilk, about a tablespoon or so at a time, to get it to the right consistency.

Oh—and some folks call 'em scallions and some say green onions. Both are green like money, so it doesn't matter, so long as it all spends the same!

MAKES 4 TO 6 SERVINGS

2 cups buttermilk pancake mix, whichever one you like

2¼ cups buttermilk, or more as needed

2 good handfuls (about 2 cups) grated sharp or mild cheddar

1 cup chopped scallions, white and green parts

½ cup (1 stick) salted butter

A li'l bit (or a lot) BBQ Pulled Pork (page 26), shredded and sauced

1 to 2 cups Juke Joint Whiskey BBQ Sauce (page 204)

1. Preheat the oven to warm or about 200°F. Place a wire rack inside a large baking sheet and set it next to the stovetop.

2. Combine the pancake mix and buttermilk in a large bowl and whisk a couple times, but don't overmix it; it should still have some lumps. Now, use a spoon to stir in the cheddar and ½ cup of the scallions. If the batter's too thick, add a little more buttermilk, about 1 tablespoon at a time.

3. Get a large cast-iron or heavy skillet hot over medium heat, about 2 minutes. Add about 2 teaspoons of the butter and let it melt; that's what's gonna give the pancakes crispy edges. Scoop up about ⅓ cup batter per pancake into the hot skillet and cook until you see a few bubbles on top and the bottom is browned and set, 2 to 3 minutes. You can cook as many pancakes as will fit, depending on how big you want them and the size of your pan. I usually use a 12-inch pan and cook two at a time.

4. Use a spatula to flip each pancake, and keep cookin' until set on the other side, about 2 more minutes. Put those pancakes on the prepared rack and place in the oven to keep warm.

5. Repeat with the rest of the batter, using more butter with each one and keeping the pancakes warm in the oven until you're ready to put it all together.

6. Wipe out the pan with a paper towel and return it to medium heat. Add a good ole amount of pork to the pan—whatever you can fit—and let it sit to crisp up on the bottom a little, 2 to 3 minutes. Now add some of your sauce—start with just a little and then add more to taste. Heat up the rest of your pork and sauce the same way.

7. Serve the pancakes with the pulled pork piled on top, drizzled with a li'l bit more sauce and topped with the remaining ½ cup scallions—because we know we need something green every day to be healthy. Amen.

DON'T NEED THIS MANY PANCAKES IN YOUR LIFE RIGHT NOW?

1. Go ahead and make the whole recipe anyway while you're at it.
2. Cool the pancakes on a rack on the counter instead of puttin' 'em in the oven to stay warm.
3. When the pancakes are cool, place them in a large freezer bag with wax paper between each one so they don't stick together.
4. Freeze until you're craving this again. Same thing with the pulled pork. You can pull out one pancake at a time (and some pork) and sop it up when you want it!
5. Heat a frozen pancake, wrapped in a paper towel, in the microwave on high until hot, 45 seconds to 1 minute.
6. Top with pulled pork and sauce and you're cookin' with gas every time!

BBQ PULLED PORK

If you don't dine with the swine, you might as well skip this page, chile, 'cuz there ain't no substitute. Now, it's not really a pork butt, y'all. The "butt" is really the shoulder of the hog. And I like to use a real heavy cast-iron pot or Dutch oven with a tight-fittin' lid for this. The cast iron lets you get a good sear on the meat and fat, and then holds that heat inside while you're braisin' the pork in the oven.

Here's the deal on the cookin' time: it's gonna depend on the size of your meat. You're gonna cook the pork until it falls apart like some of y'all relationships out there! Mm-hmm . . . But I'ma mind the business that pays me and stay out of yours! And no matter what size you use, this meat is perfect for freezing and reheating later to be used ten thousand different ways! You can make pork nachos, pork tacos, pork-stuffed baked potatoes, or pork sandwiches—the list goes on and on. If I had a dollar for every way you can use this pork, I'd be layin' on a boat in turquoise water somewhere, with an umbrella in my drink! Anyway, save that leftover meat in a big freezer bag and make somethin' else with it.

And load up your plate like they do at Saw's BBQ joint in my hometown; add it to your BBQ Baked Beans (page 156), Ole Skool Mac 'n' Cheese (page 142), or Pasta Salad (page 80), and your belly will be happy as a kid in a candy store.

MAKES 6 TO 8 SERVINGS

One 3½- to 4-pound boneless or 6- to 7½-pound bone-in pork butt (pork shoulder)

½ cup House Seasoning Blend (page 200) or Juke Joint Seasoning, or more if you've got a really big pig

½ cup canola or vegetable oil, whatever you prefer that handles high heat real good

One 32-ounce carton beef broth

3 small yellow onions, roughly chopped

3 whole garlic cloves, peeled

½ cup beef-flavored bouillon powder

½ cup (1 stick) salted butter, cut into pieces

1 tablespoon liquid smoke, to give it that real BBQ flava

Juke Joint Whiskey BBQ Sauce (page 204)

1. Put that meat on a big plate and let it come to room temperature so it'll cook evenly. Pat the meat dry with paper towels so you can also get a good sear on it.

2. Preheat the oven to 325°F.

3. With a sharp knife, score the top of the outer fat layer by making slices about 1 inch apart, about halfway through the fat only, not cutting down into the meat. Flip it around and make slices goin' the other way so it looks like a checkerboard. (Now, I don't do this to make it all cute. It makes that fat crisp up real good and lets the excess fat drain, and the meat underneath sops up all the good seasonings.)

4. Season that pig all over with the House Seasoning and get in there, flippin' that meat so you're gettin' all sides. Rub that seasonin' all up in there.

5. Heat a cast-iron pot, Dutch oven, or a heavy roasting pan over medium-high heat.

6. Add the oil to the pan, and when it's hot, carefully add the meat, fat side down, and cook on all sides until good 'n' deep brown, 2 to 3 minutes per side. Get that fat all nice and crispy! Add the broth and stir it up a little to get the good stuff off the bottom of the pan, about 1 minute. Add the onions, garlic, and bouillon and stir well. Add the butter and liquid smoke and give it another good stir.

7. Cover the pot tight and place it in the oven. Cook for 3 hours, then stick it with a fork to see if it's fallin' apart. If not, cover it back up and keep cooking until it's good 'n' done and falling apart like the lady in the front row of the *Five Heartbeats* movie. Bigger bone-in pork pieces will take up to 4 to 6 hours. The meat is done when it hits 190° to 195°F on an instant-read thermometer, or once it starts to pull apart once you've tapped it with a fork.

8. Remove from the oven, uncover, and let rest for 30 minutes.

9. Using tongs or spatulas, carefully transfer the pork to a large bowl and add some of the pan drippings and enough BBQ sauce to sop it up and make you all happy. When you think you've added enough, drizzle in more drippings and more sauce and whatever else you like, and then dig on in.

Savory
CHEESE GRITS

Hunny, we've got grits and brunch to talk about. I have a lot of thoughts about grits . . . but I don't wanna piss nobody off!

First, y'all, these are the BEST grits ever!!! Everybody always asks me how I make my grits because they are lip-smacking, high-five-ya-neighbor good! No soupy-ass grits allowed where I'm from—these are cheesy, creamy, and thick! I'll tell you, it's the bouillon that makes these taste 100 percent betta than anybody else's!

And I like sharp cheddar in mine. But you use your cheese of choice. Now, on this part, please add as much cheese as you'd like. I just eyeball mine and add a couple handfuls and then adjust as needed. I'll even empty out all the cheese in the fridge and mix it up, like cheddar, Gruyère, Swiss, and Parmesan all together. Try it before you get an opinion.

Last—and I know this is gonna be hard—but if you want, you can leave some grits so you have 'em the next day to fry up like my daddy used to do for us when we was comin' up. Or just double this recipe to make sure you got enough for brunch today and then enough to fry up for brunch tomorrow!

MAKES 4 SERVINGS

1 tablespoon chicken-flavored bouillon powder

1 tablespoon kosher salt

1 cup quick grits (yes, that's what I said)

1 cup heavy cream

2 good handfuls (about 2 cups) grated sharp cheddar

¼ cup (½ stick) salted butter, plus more for serving

½ teaspoon ground black pepper, or to taste

1. Place 4 cups water, bouillon, and salt in a big, heavy saucepan or medium pot and bring to a boil. Slowly whisk in your grits, which will keep them nice and smooth. Cover and turn the heat to low. Every now and then, take off the lid and check 'em and whisk 'em to make sure they're not sticking. They'll take about 20 minutes, even though we're using quick grits. And be careful: hot grits are like lava and they will spit while they're cookin'. Don't get burned stirrin' your pot.

2. When the grits are nice and thick and tender, add your cream and whisk to make 'em smoother and creamier. This is what my mama called "whippin' your grits." These grits are so good, y'all.

3. Then, when they're smooth and creamy, add your cheddar and keep stirring until it's good and melted and the grits are thick. Stir in the butter and pepper and adjust the seasoning to taste.

4. Serve hot, with more butter on top of each serving if you wanna!

DADDY'S FRIED CHEESE GRITS

I cannot believe that some people throw their leftover grits out. Do NOT throw these out! That is just crazy!

1. Take your grits straight outta the fridge.
2. Get a large cast-iron pan or heavy skillet good and hot over medium heat.
3. Melt a couple tablespoons butter in the pan.
4. With a large spoon, portion out the grits, 2 to 3 tablespoons at a time, and cook on both sides until heated through and browned, turning once, 4 to 5 minutes.
5. Eat hot with some Yeasted Drop Biscuits (page 35) and lotsa salted butter and crisp bacon. That tastes like the South, y'all! Yum!

SHRIMP 'n' GRITS

I mean, what more needs to be said?

This dish is most definitely a southern staple, but I managed to add a little twist here: you take some leftover smoked turkey leg meat, and it's gonna work your entire world. The savory, creamy sauce and my cheese grits make the perfect pair. It's almost like kissing cousins. You can find smoked turkey legs at your local grocery store.

MAKES 2 TO 3 SERVINGS

Savory Cheese Grits (page 29)

For the sauce
¼ cup (½ stick) salted butter
½ medium yellow onion, diced
½ bell pepper, chopped
2 tablespoons all-purpose flour

2 tablespoons Cajun seasoning, or more if you want
1 tablespoon chicken-flavored bouillon powder
2 teaspoons paprika (for color)
1 tablespoon garlic powder
1 tablespoon onion powder

½ pound shrimp, peeled and deveined
Meat from 1 smoked turkey leg, cut into pieces (see headnote)
Chopped fresh parsley, for garnish (optional)

1. Go ahead and cook your grits, since they tend to take longer than the sauce.

2. To make the sauce, heat a large pan over medium heat, then add the butter. Once the butter is melted, add the onion and pepper and cook until soft, 3 to 4 minutes.

3. Add the flour and mix until the flour has completely coated the veggies. Slowly add in 3 cups water, whisking constantly to prevent the gravy from clumping.

4. Bring to a simmer and then add the Cajun seasoning, bouillon, paprika, and garlic and onion powders. Taste and adjust to your liking—remember, bland food ain't ever been in style, hunny.

5. Let the sauce thicken for 2 to 3 minutes, then add your shrimp and turkey meat. Cook until the shrimp turn pink, 4 to 5 minutes.

6. Serve the grits with the sauce on top. Don't be stingy with the meat! Be sure to add those chunks of smoked turkey to the bowl. Sprinkle with a little parsley if you want to make folks think you did something special and serve immediately!

Danni's Juke Joint Comfort Food

YEASTED DROP BISCUITS
with Butta

OK, we're baking now, so you gotta measure your dry ingredients more carefully, using the flat, back edge of a knife to level them off in the measuring cup or spoon once you scoop 'em outta the package.

I use bread flour for these biscuits because it's got a higher protein content that gives structure to yeasted breads. You can use all-purpose flour, though, if that's what you got. But know that the texture of your batter will be a little wetter; just add more flour a teaspoon at a time until the batter is tacky but not sticky.

I scoop these drop biscuits into two heavy cast-iron skillets to rise and then bake, because that makes the bottoms crispy, just like I like 'em. But you can scoop and bake these on a large ungreased baking sheet or in a lightly greased big casserole dish.

MAKES 20 BISCUITS

5 cups bread flour

One ¼-ounce envelope (2¼ teaspoons) active dry yeast

3 tablespoons sugar

1 tablespoon plus 2 teaspoons baking powder

2 teaspoons kosher salt

1 teaspoon baking soda

½ cup (1 stick) salted butter, frozen

5 tablespoons butter-flavored shortening (I use Crisco), plus more for greasing

2¾ cups plus 2 tablespoons buttermilk

Butta of your choice (see page 205)

I. Stir together the flour, yeast, sugar, baking powder, salt, and baking soda in a large bowl. Using a cheese grater, roughly grate the butter into the dry ingredients. With your fingers, crumble the shortening into the bowl and mix it and the butter into the dry ingredients until the mixture resembles small peas. *recipe continues*

35

2. Heat 2¾ cups of the buttermilk in a small saucepan over medium-low heat until it's warm like a baby's bottle, between 108° and 110°F, about 2 minutes. (You can check the temperature if you have a cooking thermometer.) Don't go any hotter than that or the yeast ain't gonna work and your biscuits gonna be flat. Add the milk to the flour mixture and lightly mix with a fork just enough to make a smooth dough. Don't overmix it!

3. If you don't wanna make all these biscuits now, the dough can be divided at this point, wrapped in plastic, and kept in the fridge for a couple days.

4. Lightly grease two cast-iron skillets or a large casserole dish with the shortening. (You can also use one large baking sheet, *but don't grease it— it'll burn if you do*.)

5. Using a ¼-cup ice cream scoop or measuring cup, scoop the dough into the prepared skillets. Lightly brush the tops with the remaining 2 tablespoons buttermilk and lightly cover with plastic wrap. Let rise for 30 minutes.

6. Meanwhile, preheat the oven to 425°F with a rack in the middle.

7. Bake the biscuits until golden brown on the tops and sides, 20 to 22 minutes. This longer cooking time ensures that the biscuits are light and crispy on the outside and cooked through, soft, and pillowy on the inside.

8. Remove from the oven and I dare you not to eat three smeared with any one of my amazing flavored buttas standing up over the sink. (Or in the words of Diddy, "Can't stop, won't stop.")

Danni's Juke Joint Comfort Food

LEFTOVER BISCUITS

For those rare times when I have leftover cooked biscuits, I'll freeze them to serve later.

1. Individually wrap leftover biscuits (as if you're gonna have any left!) in plastic wrap. Put the wrapped biscuits into a freezer bag and freeze.

2. Later, place the wrapped, frozen biscuits on the counter to thaw for about 30 minutes.

3. Pop in the microwave, still in the plastic wrap, and cook on high until heated through, 35 to 45 seconds.

4. Carefully unwrap and serve with lotsa butta.

Cake Mix
CINNAMON ROLLS

Now, this one takes the CAKE! Literally, hunny!

Cinnamon rolls are one of my favorite things to eat. Homemade or store-bought, I want them!

My auntie Joann is considered the baker in our family. And she does a really great job . . . usually. She was the head cook at a school in Jacksonville, Florida, and ran their cafeteria, and she was known for her amazing cinnamon rolls. One summer when I was staying at her house, I asked her to make those rolls. I was anticipating them all day. But when I took a bite: chile, she had added *raisins*. I was not ready for that, nor did I like it. She told me, "A cinnamon roll ain't a cinnamon roll without raisins." Well, little did she know, one day I would come up with something better.

I know cinnamon rolls can be pretty tedious to make or intimidating, even for the best baker. But don't you fret, I have found an easy way to do it! I know that this recipe is a hit, because I used to sell these cinnamon rolls back in the day to support my daughter and myself. And let me tell ya, I sold out each time.

All you need are four ingredients to make the dough: cake mix, water, flour, and instant yeast. No added salt, eggs, or milk, none of that! And you can change the flavor by simply changing up your cake mix: lemon, chocolate, red velvet, birthday cake, you name it!

For the dough

5 cups all-purpose flour, plus more for kneading

1 box vanilla cake mix (or other cake mix of your choice)

4½ cups warm water (108° to 110°F)

¼ cup instant yeast

For the filling

1 cup (2 sticks) salted butter, at room temperature

2 cups packed brown sugar

2 tablespoons ground cinnamon

1 teaspoon kosher salt (optional; I think it brings out the flavors more)

For the icing

One 8-ounce block cream cheese, at room temperature

½ cup (1 stick) salted butter, at room temperature

3 cups powdered sugar

Chopped pecans, for topping (optional)

I. To make the dough: If you have a stand mixer, combine the flour, cake mix, water, and yeast in the bowl and mix on medium speed with a dough hook for 5 to 6 minutes, until smooth. Then skip ahead to Step 6.

2. If you are not using a stand mixer, put the ingredients into a large bowl and mix with a wooden spoon until combined, 3 to 4 minutes tops. The dough will be tacky, but that's what you want! If it seems a bit dry, just add a little water, 1 tablespoon at a time, until it reaches the right consistency.

3. Spread about 2 tablespoons flour on a clean countertop.

4. Transfer the dough to the floured surface and bring it in together with your hands so it starts to form into a ball, then knead the dough with the heel of your hand. You wanna make a back-and-forth rocking motion, like you're in a rocking chair, but with your hands instead.

5. Do this until the dough starts to look like a nice smooth ball, 3 to 5 minutes. (It's not gonna be completely smooth, and that's OK.)

6. Put the dough in a large, clean bowl, cover with a kitchen towel or plastic wrap, and set it aside to rest until doubled in size, about 30 minutes. Let this dough rest like the Lord did on the seventh day! Leave it be.

7. While the dough is resting, go ahead and make your filling: Combine the butter, brown sugar, cinnamon, and salt (if using) in a medium bowl and mix together until all the ingredients are blended like a family!

8. Once the dough has doubled in size, dust your counter with 2 more tablespoons flour and place the dough on the surface. Using your hands, press the dough out into a rectangle about ½ inch thick; no need for a rolling pin.

9. Use a butter knife to spread the filling on the dough. Make sure you get all the way to the edges.

10. Roll the dough into a log and cut it into 12 pieces, about an inch thick. We like them big in my house!

11. Set the cinnamon rolls on a parchment-lined baking sheet, cover again with a kitchen towel or plastic wrap, and let rise for 20 minutes. The second rise lets the dough relax from all the work you just did to it.

12. Preheat the oven to 350°F.

13. Bake the rolls for 15 to 20 minutes. Check them around the 15-minute mark—if the center seems cooked, it's OK to take them out of the oven. A tad undercooked is OK, too, because the rolls will continue to cook a little once they are removed from the oven.

14. While the rolls are baking, make your icing: Put the cream cheese and butter in a large bowl and beat with a hand mixer for 1 minute (or use a whisk if you want to burn some calories!). Add the powdered sugar 1 cup at a time, mixing after each addition.

15. When the rolls are done, let cool for about 10 minutes before adding the icing.

16. Spread the icing on the rolls and top with the pecans (if using). Please enjoy while warm! These should be ooey, gooey, tender, and fluffy rolls! You can always freeze the leftover rolls for another time, but let them cool completely first.

TIPS FOR MAKING CINNAMON ROLLS

- Don't overmix the dough. You want to be gentle with this dough but also work pretty fast. The dough has a lot of gluten, so the more you knead it, the tougher it will be. You want soft, slightly chewy, fluffy, melt-in-your-mouth rolls.

- Do not use extremely hot water for the dough; it can kill the yeast and the dough will not rise. You want it lukewarm (108° to 110°F), like a baby's bottle temperature.

- Let the dough rest! This is important; if you let the dough rest properly, the rolls will be light and airy.

- Be sure to not add too much filling to the rolls. You can get creative, though—for example, try using my Cinnamon Crunch Butta (page 206) for additional flava in your filling.

STACKED BANANA PUDDING PANCAKES
with Sopped-Up Butter Syrup

Banana pudding is one of my favorite desserts, and now we're gonna eat it for breakfast. Because why not? Life is all about taking risks, and I like to jump first and ask questions lata, OK?

And you're just gonna start the recipe that's on the pancake box you got. Every box is different, and you know what you like. One quick word, though, y'all: use buttermilk instead of water or regular milk to make them extra fluffy! Make your syrup first and then the pudding, and the pancakes last so everythin' will be ready to eat at the same time.

My mama likes her pancakes thin as a bad lace-front wig. If that's you, then just add some extra buttermilk to thin 'em out. Me, I like 'em good 'n' plump so they can grab ahold of all that banana pudding and butta syrup!

MAKES 10 TO 12 PANCAKES

Sopped-up butter syrup

½ cup (1 stick) salted butter
1 cup sugar
½ cup whole milk
½ teaspoon baking soda
½ teaspoon kosher salt
1 teaspoon pure vanilla extract

Pudding filling

One 8-ounce block cream cheese, at room temperature
One 8-ounce container Cool Whip
½ of a 14-ounce can sweetened condensed milk (that's just shy of 1 cup)

Pancakes

2 cups crushed Nilla wafers (that's 45 cookies, y'all, if you're countin', or about ½ of an 11-ounce box)
2 cups pancake mix, whateva type you like best
2½ cups buttermilk
1 large banana, thinly sliced
½ cup (1 stick) salted butter, for the pan
Sweetened whipped cream or Cool Whip, for serving
Powdered sugar, for serving

45

1. This syrup is so easy to make, y'all. First up, you're gonna melt the butter in a medium pot over medium-high heat. Make sure it's big enough because we're gonna bring this up to a boil in a minute and you don't want it spilling over. Add the sugar and milk, whisk it up, and bring the mixture to a boil. Set your timer and let it boil for 2 minutes to get all foamy. Remove from the heat and let the bubbles settle a little bit, about 1 minute.

2. Add the baking soda, salt, and vanilla. It's gonna be so delicious, it'll taste good on Joe's toenails! Set it aside till you're ready to eat.

3. Now we're gonna make our filling, which is the easiest thing you've ever done. Place your cream cheese, Cool Whip, and condensed milk in a large bowl. Using a hand mixer on medium speed, mix until smooth. (Gotta use your mixer for this, 'cuz if you try to stir this all by hand, hunny, you be there lookin' crazy while you try to get this all nice and smooth. You don't want any lumps or else people be talkin' 'bout you, sayin', "Girl, what that was?" You don't need that!) Put that bowl to the side and get on with the pancakes.

4. To make your pancakes, first thing, crush up those Nilla wafer cookies. Put 'em in a heavy freezer bag, seal it, and whack it real good with the bottom of a frying pan or push down on 'em with the bottom of a heavy bowl. You can leave 'em a little chunky if you like. Save half for topping your pancakes on the plates.

5. Preheat the oven to warm or about 200°F. Place a wire rack inside a large baking sheet next to the stovetop.

6. Combine the pancake mix and buttermilk in a large bowl. Whisk it a couple times, but don't overmix it. Add half your crushed cookies and get 'em all good and sopped up in there. Fold in the banana slices. And if you don't like banana, hunny, you don't have to add them. These pancakes are gonna be so good with just those cookies all up in there.

7. Get a large cast-iron or heavy skillet hot over medium heat, about 2 minutes. Add about 2 teaspoons butter and let it melt; that's what's gonna give the pancakes crispy edges.

8. Spoon a heaping ¼ cup batter—or more if you like—into the pan and let it sit until bubbles start to pop on top and the bottom is browned and set, 2 to 3 minutes. You can cook as many pancakes as will fit, depending on how big you want them and the size of your pan. I usually use a 12-inch pan and cook two at a time. Flip it over with a spatula and cook on the other side until golden brown and cooked through, 1½ to 2 minutes. Put that pancake on the rack and place in the oven to keep warm while cookin' the rest of the batter and gettin' everything ready.

recipe continues

9. Repeat with the rest of the batter, using more butter with each one and then keeping the pancakes warm in the oven until you're ready to put it all together.

10. To serve, place 1 pancake on a large plate and sop it up real good with syrup, 'cuz you don't want that to be dry. Then put some of that good pudding down, add some of the remaining cookie crumbs, and top with another pancake.

Keep puttin' pancakes down with the syrup and pudding to make sure it's all sopped up and everybody be wantin' to come eat at your house.

11. Drizzle with more butter syrup and top with some whipped cream and powdered sugar, if you want it more fabulous. Go big or go home, hunny—that's the way to do it!

TIPS FOR MAKING
TALK-OF-THE-TOWN PANCAKES

- I'm a pancake girl, so you'll see three pancake recipes in this book. And yes, I use store-bought pancake mix, 'cuz nobody got time to be makin' up all that stuff. You know that stuff is good, hunny, because I also use it to make my Spatchcocked Whole Fried Chicken (page 113). Yes, that's right. On my fried chicken. That's how much I love the flavor of pancakes!

- Use whatever brand you like best. Just make sure you follow the directions on the box, because every brand is a little different and uses different amounts of liquid. Some call for water, milk, or buttermilk; some add melted butter or oil; and some even add an egg or two.

- In some of my pancake recipes I use whole milk; in others I use buttermilk. You do you. If you do substitute buttermilk, you will need a little bit more than if you're usin' whole milk or water, 'cuz buttermilk's thicker. But I like that whole other taste buttermilk gives food.

- Buttermilk also will make a thicker batter; thin it a little as needed, an extra tablespoon or so at a time.

- Keep your first pancakes warm in a low oven (about 200°F) while you're finishing the batter. It's best to put them on a wire rack set over a big baking sheet. That way, they're good 'n' hot when everything is ready.

- Dependin' on what I'm servin' 'em with, I make my pancakes all different ways. You can add sliced bananas and smashed cookies (like in my Stacked Banana Pudding Pancakes on page 45) or fresh berries or chocolate chips if you like sweet. And try my savory Cheddar & Scallion Pancakes (page 23) to give you ideas for your own main-thang kinda meal.

- Another secret to tender, fluffy pancakes: don't overmix when adding the wet to the dry! Gently fold it all together. Lumps are OK. And use lotsa butta in your pan to get those edges crispy!

CHEF SALAD
with Saltine Crackers

I live in bougie LA now—where they think a brunch salad should be made with kale (*no*). If it's up to me, this is the salad I want at brunch while I'm sippin' on my mimosa! This recipe was inspired by a place called Top That Grille, a neighborhood joint where I grew up that made the best salads in the hood. You'd walk in—since the drive-thru speaker was sometimes broken—and be greeted by chocolate women with short hair and gold teeth in the front. Their hair was always laid but in a hairnet for food safety. But could they make a salad, hunny! And you'd watch 'em make it right in front of you. That chef salad was loaded with simple things, and their ranch dressing was what *made it*! The salads were served with a pack of saltines for you to crumble on top. Now, they weren't the only place that made chef salads. But they were the only place that got it right *every single time*. And that's 'cuz they made it with a lot of love and laughter. Thinkin' back on that place, this is what I call a true Birmingham Westside salad—and a tribute to those ladies.

MAKES 1 SALAD

3 handfuls (2 to 3 cups) shredded iceberg lettuce

1 cup cooked tricolor pasta (optional)

2 handfuls (about 1½ cups) diced tomatoes

⅓ cup diced red or white onion

1 hard-boiled egg, peeled and chopped (see How to Hard-Boil Eggs, page 65)

1 good handful (about 1 cup) grated cheddar

½ cup chopped cooked bacon or store-bought bacon bits

Juke Joint Ranch Dressing (page 202)

A few saltine crackers, for serving

1. Place the lettuce in a large salad bowl. Top with the pasta (if using), tomatoes, onion, and boiled egg, going all around to make it pretty. Then top with the cheese and bacon. Drizzle with as much ranch dressing as you want and crumble those saltines over the top.

2. Toss it all around and enjoy with a mimosa!

Pineapple Mimosa
POUND CAKE

This is the perfect cake to make to soak up all those mimosas at brunch. That's right . . . you can never have too many, even if the mimosa is in your cake. This cake is dense like a traditional pound cake but melts in your mouth like a butter cake, with a bit of a sweet, boozy flava at the end.

MAKES 1 BUNDT CAKE, 12 TO 16 SERVINGS

For the cake
- 1½ cups (3 sticks) salted butter, at room temperature
- 5 large eggs, at room temperature
- 2 cups sugar
- 3 cups cake flour (see Baking Tips, page 171)
- 1 teaspoon kosher salt
- ¼ cup heavy cream
- 1 cup Champagne or Prosecco
- One 8-ounce can crushed pineapple, drained (but keep the juice for the glaze)

For the glaze
- 1 cup powdered sugar
- 2 tablespoons reserved pineapple juice
- 2 tablespoons Champagne or Prosecco

I. Preheat the oven to 325°F. Grab a Bundt pan and spray it generously with cooking spray to make sure that cake comes out CLEAN!

2. To make the cake: Combine the butter and one of the eggs in a large mixing bowl and beat together with a hand mixer on medium speed. Add the sugar and 2 more eggs and mix together until combined. You don't wanna overwork your cake batter—that's gonna make it dry—so be sure to mix for only about 20 seconds in between each addition.

3. Add 1 cup of the flour and mix for about 20 seconds. Again, don't overwork it! Add 1 more egg, mix again, then 1 more cup of flour, then the last egg, and the remaining 1 cup flour, beating after each addition and ending with the flour. Mix until creamy.

4. Now add the heavy cream and Champagne and beat for about 15 seconds just to incorporate the liquid into the batter. Gently fold in the crushed pineapple.

5. Evenly distribute the batter in the prepared pan, spreading it with a small spatula or butter knife. Tap the pan on the counter three times to allow the cake to settle in the pan and eliminate any air bubbles that can dry the cake out when it's baking (chile, we don't need those problems!).

6. Bake until a toothpick inserted in the middle of the cake comes out clean, about 1 hour and 15 minutes.

7. Let the cake cool in the pan for about 15 minutes or so.

8. While the cake is cooling, let's make the glaze: Add the powdered sugar, pineapple juice, and Champagne to a medium bowl and whisk until smooth.

9. Unmold the cake onto a plate. Let the cake cool for about an hour. Drizzle the glaze over the cake and let it sit to harden slightly, about 10 minutes or so. Cut and serve!

SOMETHIN'
TO SNACK ON

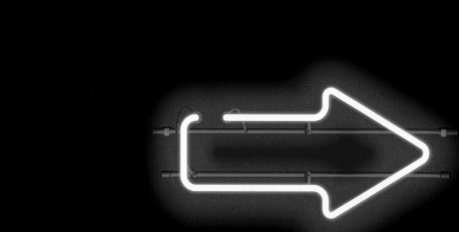

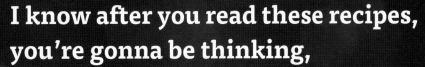

I know after you read these recipes, you're gonna be thinking,

"Chile, ain't no way this is just a snack!" Yes, each of these could be a whole meal, but food is what you make it. And where I'm from, this is our version of a snack. Whenever you walk into somebody's house, they always got somethin' to snack on: you've got some spicy nuts out, a pound cake (cake is always a snack, by the way), cheese, crackers. Y'all know I didn't get these hips by eatin' grapes and honeydew!

I don't know about y'all, but when I go out to a restaurant, most of the time, bread is the appetizer. And in the South, there's a good chance they're gonna set down a bowl of mini cornbread muffins when you get there. No one ever skips those!

Club Meetin'
CHICKEN SALAD

First off, everybody knows chicken salad is a snack, not a main course! And in my family, we eat this anytime. My mama has a longtime girlfriend named Jessie, and she is known for her salad in the city! I'm gonna tell you this is *the best chicken salad you've ever eaten!* She makes it perfect every time, so I called her a few years ago and got her to give me her secrets. First, we startin' from scratch with a whole chicken. Yes, you heard me right. Please do not use canned chicken, precooked chicken, or boneless chicken breasts, because it will not taste the same, mm-kay?

The key to makin' good chicken salad is usin' the whole bird—thighs, legs, breasts, and wings—and pickin' all the meat off it. Cook your chicken in a big pot that can hold it and enough water to cover by 2 inches. Your cooking time will depend on the size of your chicken. If yours is bigger than 4 pounds, then add an additional 15 minutes cooking time per pound. The meat should be falling apart.

In the words of Auntie Jessie, "That's yo' chicken salad!" Meaning: the base of the chicken salad is all about the seasoning, hunny—what's in the pot with the chicken matters. Don't be afraid to season; now is not the time to hold back. Plus, the stock you'll get from the chicken will taste amazing! Save it for later to make gravies or stews or boil your rice in it.

Duke's PAID

Disco Ladies's — Fish Pla
collec

Miriam - 100.00

Zelma - 100.00

Lane - 15.00

Pam - Owe

Jem. 50

Phyliss -

1 whole chicken, about 4 pounds

¼ cup chicken-flavored bouillon powder

¼ cup garlic powder

¼ cup onion powder

¼ cup plus 1 teaspoon paprika (not that smoky kind, OK?)

2 tablespoons kosher salt

One 10-ounce bag frozen chopped onion and pepper blend

4 large eggs, at room temperature

One 16-ounce jar sweet salad cubes or sweet pickle relish, or to taste

2 cups mayonnaise (I like Duke's)

⅓ cup sugar, or mo' or less, however you like it

Sandwich bread, Saltines, or Ritz crackers, for serving

I. Place the whole chicken in your favorite big pot with enough water to cover it by 2 inches. Add the bouillon, garlic and onion powders, ¼ cup of the paprika, and the salt. Don't eva be afraid to season, hunny; trust yourself. Just remember, a little at a time—you can always add, but you can't take away. Then add the frozen onion and pepper mixture.

2. Bring the mixture to a boil, then reduce the heat to medium and simmer for 30 minutes. Carefully taste your broth by dippin' into it with a spoon. Adjust your seasonings to taste and then let it keep cookin' until the chicken is really tender and cooked through, about 1½ hours. About 10 minutes before you think the chicken is done, add those eggs to the pot to get all hard-boiled.

3. If you're like me, you're gonna wanna save this good broth, so put a big pot in the sink and set your colander on top before you drain

the bird. That way, you'll catch all that flava to use later for somethin' else! Drain that chicken and the eggs in the colander and let sit until cool enough to handle. Discard the onions and peppers.

4. When the bird is cool enough to handle, remove and discard the skin. Pull the meat from the bones and put it in a large bowl. This chicken is so tender from the way we cooked it, it won't need shreddin'.

5. Peel and finely chop the eggs. (See my easy tip: No Peelin' Hard-Boiled Eggs on page 65.)

6. Add the eggs, sweet salad cubes, mayonnaise, sugar, and the remaining 1 teaspoon paprika to the chicken and stir well to combine. Adjust the seasoning to taste the way you like it, cover, and refrigerate until ready to serve.

7. Spread on sandwich bread or crackers.

Cajun
DEVILED EGGS

Just like pasta salad and potato salad, deviled eggs are served at every Black cookout, wedding, baby shower, and holiday! They can make or break any of these occasions. Show up to a function with these made wrong, and you are asking for a fresh can of whoop-ass. There is always one person in each family who only does one special dish. You have a person who makes the dressing, another who makes the mac 'n' cheese, and you got a person who makes the potato salad or deviled eggs. And don't you DARE forget the paprika! Not the smoky stuff—use regular, bland-tasting paprika. It's just for decoration, hunny.

And let me tell ya, makin' deviled eggs ain't no easy job—it's bravery at its finest, if you ask me. My family and I like 'em a little sweet, so just like the potato salad, you gotta add a little pinch of sugar, too. That's the secret. It just balances everything out. Trust me. Now, these have a little kick to them—they aren't traditional, but they are always a hit.

I like to add a little cooked shrimp on top, or you could even add lump crabmeat if ya really trying to slide! If adding shrimp, you can cook your own or use precooked; season them with a little seafood seasoning and then lay them on top of the prepared eggs.

MAKES 6 SERVINGS

12 large eggs

½ cup mayonnaise (I like Duke's)

⅓ cup sweet salad cubes, sweet pickle relish, or gherkin pickles cut into small pieces

1 to 2 tablespoons yellow mustard, depending on how tangy you want it, but I'd start with one

2 teaspoons sugar

2 teaspoons House Seasoning Blend (page 200), Juke Joint Black Cajun Seasoning, or Juke Joint Seasoning, or more to taste

¼ teaspoon cayenne

1 tablespoon dried parsley

1 teaspoon paprika

1. Boil and peel your eggs the right way—see How to Hard-Boil Eggs (page 65) and No Peelin' Hard-Boiled Eggs (page 65)—and then you'll be ready to pick up here. (Or you can boil and peel your eggs your way, even though my way is better.)

2. Remove the yolks from the halved eggs and place them in a large bowl. (You should see creamy gold!) Mash the yolks with a fork.

3. Add the mayonnaise, sweet salad cubes, mustard, sugar, seasoning, and cayenne and mix well. Taste and adjust that thang like you like it—more mustard, more seasonings, and so on. If you want it creamier, add a tad more mayo.

4. Lay the egg halves on a platter, and using a spoon, scoop some of the filling into each half. Sprinkle the eggs with the parsley and paprika to make 'em look all pretty. Refrigerate for about an hour, or you can eat them right away! And get ready for everyone to assign you a new job!

HOW TO HARD-BOIL EGGS

I know there are a lot of folks who don't know how to boil an egg. I'm not gonna call no names, but some of y'all boil them to DEATH. With that green snotty yolk, phew! That ain't gonna cut it, and my mama always said, "If ya know betta, ya do betta." You want a nice hard-boil, with a beautiful canary-yellow yolk. Smooth and creamy is what we want. So here is a way to get perfect boiled eggs.

1. Add the eggs to a large pot, fill with water to cover by an inch or two, and add 1 tablespoon of salt. (This will help the eggshells come off more easily.)
2. Bring the eggs to a *high* boil, *not* a simmer!
3. Once the water starts to boil, remove from the heat. Set aside, with the lid on, for 14 minutes. Please set a timer—this is really important.
4. While the eggs are doing their thing, fill a large bowl with water and ice to make an ice bath for the eggs once they're done.
5. Once the timer is done, pour the hot water off the eggs.
6. Put the eggs into the ice bath to cool completely—about 30 minutes—before you try to peel them.
7. And now go read my tip below—No Peelin' Hard-Boiled Eggs.

NO PEELIN' HARD-BOILED EGGS

Once you start using this trick to peel your eggs, you'll start eating more of them!

1. Cut your hard-boiled eggs in half lengthwise on a cutting board.
2. With a teaspoon, scoop along the shell of each half, and then plop it out, keeping the white and yolk together in a perfect half. Yes, it's that easy!

CARAMELIZED FRENCH ONION DIP
with Chicken-Fried Potato Chips

When I was growing up, my mama and her girlfriends would always have Ruffles potato chips and French onion dip to snack on at their social savings club meetings. Hunny, if you don't know what a social savings club is, let me explain.

In our culture, social savings clubs are women's groups that meet monthly to eat, gossip, pay dues, and plan parties and fundraisers. The club's purpose is to raise money all year, doin' things like selling fish plates, candy, calendars, and throwin' their parties. At the end of the year, they'd divide all that money they made among themselves. It was a way to support their financial goals. Every club would have a really fun name, too. My mama and her girlfriends called themselves the "Disco Ladies."

And BABY, did they party! Folks will buy a ticket to a social savings club party for a li'l of nothing, like twenty-five bucks—all you can eat and all you can DRANK! Some parties were held at my daddy's juke joint, and some were even BYOB; a few were held at a popular Birmingham place called Leonard's Night Club. Hunny, EVERYBODY had a party at that place. Folks would get dressed to the nines for the parties. I'm talkin' fur coats, sequined dresses, kitten heels, shoulder pads, red lipstick, and so much White Diamond perfume it would set the place on fire if you lit a match!

French onion dip was even on the menu for those big parties; that's how super popular it was! To me as a little girl, this was so yummy, and it's still one of my favorite dip flavors. And to all those social savings club ladies: thank you for showing me the value of sisterhood and what it means to really live life to the fullest!

French onion dip

¼ cup (½ stick) salted butter

1 large sweet onion, such as Vidalia (you want the sweet onion, trust me), diced

One 8-ounce block cream cheese, at room temperature

1 cup sour cream

3 tablespoons House Seasoning Blend (page 200) or Juke Joint Seasoning

2 tablespoons dried parsley

Chicken-fried potato chips

2 large Russet potatoes, peeled

Canola or vegetable oil, for frying

2 large eggs

2 cups all-purpose flour

¼ cup House Seasoning Blend (page 200) or Juke Joint Seasoning

3 tablespoons cornstarch

Kosher salt, for sprinkling

I. Make your dip first so it can be chillin' in the fridge at least 1 hour before serving: You gotta caramelize the onion or else it ain't gonna be sopped up, y'all! And it takes patience to get 'em right by slowly cookin' 'em! Add the butter to a large skillet and start to melt it over medium-high heat. Add the onion (the butta doesn't need to be melted all the way), stir a little, and—this is a really important step—cover with a lid. Cook until the onion is soft, about 5 minutes, then uncover, stir, and continue to cook, stirring every couple minutes, until they're nice and deep brown, 20 to 30 minutes. If your onion starts to burn or cook too fast, drop that heat down low like an Uncle Luke's Peep Show, hunny, and add a coupla teaspoons water. It'll be fine.

2. Once the onion is cooked, remove it from the heat and let them cool completely. Meanwhile, combine the cream cheese, sour cream, seasoning, and dried parsley in a large bowl and mix well. Add the cooled onion and adjust the seasoning to taste. Cover and refrigerate for at least 1 hour before serving, or up to 24 hours.

3. Now, let's fry some chips real quick! First things first: You want these potato chips to be as thin as you can get them. But, please, Lord, don't hurt yourself. If you wanna use a mandoline, you can; if you don't have one, that's OK, too. Just use a heavy, sharp knife and slice the potatoes as thin as you can.

4. Place the sliced potatoes in a bowl of cold water. This keeps the potatoes from turning brown too soon and removes the starches, so that they get nice and crispy.

5. Add enough oil to come halfway up the sides of a large, heavy pot or deep-fat fryer and heat it to 350°F over medium-high heat. When your oil is shimmering, it's ready.

6. Place a wire rack inside a large baking sheet and set it next to the stovetop.

7. Drain the potato slices well in a colander and lightly pat dry.

8. Meanwhile, to make your chicken fry coating, whisk the eggs with 2 tablespoons water in a large bowl.

9. Combine the flour, seasoning, and cornstarch in a second large bowl and whisk with a fork to combine.

10. Working in batches, toss the potato slices first in the eggs to lightly coat, and then into the flour mixture to coat on all sides.

11. Again working in batches, shake off any excess coating back into the bowl and gently lay the battered potatoes one at a time into the hot oil going away from you (not dropping them)—so they won't spatter. Don't overcrowd your pan or these'll steam instead of turning golden brown. Fry, stirring with a long-handled fork to prevent the chips from sticking together, until golden brown on both sides and the potatoes are cooked through and float to the top, about 5 minutes.

12. Transfer to the prepared wire rack to drain and sprinkle lightly with salt. Repeat with the remaining potatoes, letting the oil return to 350°F before adding new batches to the oil.

13. Chips are done! Put the dip in a pretty bowl, make a batch of dranks, and thank the Disco Ladies for inspiring one of the best dips of your life!

BACON & CHEESE HUSH PUPPIES
with Juke Joint Ranch Dressing

I swear, y'all, I just love makin' fried food. It's so comforting to me. It sounds like food rain while it's cookin', and the smell is just the best!

You're not making these hush puppies like you'd make regular cornbread. This recipe doesn't use eggs, and I put in a few handfuls of cheese and lots of my good Cajun seasoning blend for big, bold flavor. I make my hush puppies large, but you can make 'em smaller, if that's your style—adjust your cooking time if you make small ones.

These can be frozen in a freezer bag once they've cooled to room temperature. Pop them in a 350°F oven while still frozen for about 15 minutes, or reheat in an air fryer.

MAKES 15 TO 20 HUSH PUPPIES, 4 TO 6 SERVINGS

2 boxes Jiffy corn muffin mix (I like the sweetness the Jiffy mix gives these hush puppies)

½ cup self-rising flour

2 tablespoons Juke Joint Black Cajun Seasoning or other Cajun seasoning

One 8-ounce block cream cheese, at room temperature

2 cups buttermilk or whole milk

2 handfuls (about 2 cups) grated sharp cheddar

1½ handfuls (about 1½ cups) grated mozzarella

¾ cup chopped scallions, green parts only

8 strips cooked bacon, crumbled

Canola or vegetable oil, for frying

Kosher salt, for sprinkling

Juke Joint Ranch Dressing (page 202)

I. Place a wire rack inside a large baking sheet and set it near the stovetop.

2. Combine the muffin mix, flour, and Cajun seasoning in a large bowl and stir well. Plop in the cream cheese and just let it be. Don't stir till I tell you to! Add the buttermilk, those handfuls of cheese, ½ cup of the scallions, and the bacon

(just because we're addin' greens to this, girl, doesn't mean we gettin' all vegan!) and then start gettin' your exercise. This batter is thick, almost like a biscuit dough, y'all, and you gotta get to it and turn it around with a fork, heavy wooden spoon, or rubber spatula. You can do it, put your back into it—stir it all around!

recipe continues

3. Add enough oil to come halfway up the sides of a large, heavy pot or deep-fat fryer and heat it to 350°F over medium-high heat. (If you're using a deep fryer, take out the basket so the batter doesn't stick to it.) When your oil is shimmering, it's ready. You can also simply drop in a teaspoon of batter, and if it sizzles, it's ready!

4. With a medium ice cream scoop (about ¼ cup), drop the batter into the hot oil in batches, 5 or 6 at a time. You don't want to overcrowd these—we're not at the Million Man March! You want these to be the same size and cook evenly. And please do not undercook the batter! If you do, you ain't gonna have nothin' but a pile of fried mush, and then they be talkin' about you in the group chat, and you don't want that. Same thing about overcookin'—if you overcook the hush puppies, they'll be tough and dry as a muddy work boot.

5. Just make sure you're stirring them with a long-handled slotted spoon or a big fork so they cook on all sides. The point is to cook them through on the inside and at the same time to get 'em crisp and golden brown, 4 to 5 minutes in that hot grease Jacuzzi. Take 'em out when they float to the top, and put them on the prepared wire rack. Sprinkle lightly with salt.

6. Allow the oil to return to 350°F and repeat with the remaining batter.

7. To serve, place the hush puppies on a big platter, garnish with the remaining ¼ cup scallions and a big bowl of Juke Joint Ranch for dippin', and then try not to bite your hand off when you're eatin', they're so good!

FRIED DILL PICKLE SPEARS

I know you've seen fried dill pickle chips or slices before. I use long spears for my fried pickles, and I shallow fry them in a large cast-iron skillet. You can use a bigger pot or Dutch oven—just increase the amount of oil.

I like my pickles to be fried hard and crispy . . . so crispy they make you think of those hard waterfall and finger wave hairstyles we wore back in the '90s. You can fry a couple at a time, but remember, no frying spa . . . don't overcrowd the pan. Cook as many as you would like and serve them with that bomb-ass Juke Joint Ranch Dressing and a side of hot sauce. They're perfect every single time.

MAKES 4 SERVINGS

Canola or vegetable oil, for frying
3 large eggs

2½ cups Homemade Fish Fry (page 201), Juke Joint Fish Fry, or whatever Louisiana-style fish fry you've got in your neck of the woods

12 dill pickle spears, patted dry on paper towels (so the batter will stick)
Juke Joint Ranch Dressing (page 202)

1. Add enough oil to come about 2 inches up the sides of a large cast-iron skillet and heat it to 360°F over medium-high heat.

2. Place a wire rack inside a large baking sheet and set it next to the stovetop.

3. Beat the eggs in a medium bowl.

4. Place the fish fry in a large freezer bag.

5. Working in batches, dip the pickles into the eggs to lightly coat and then place them in the fish fry bag. Seal the bag and shake real good so they've got somethin' to wear in the oil Jacuzzi.

6. Remove the pickles from the fry bag, shake to remove any excess, and gently lay them into the hot oil, being careful not to overcrowd the pan (that brings down the temperature and makes your food steam instead of crisp!). Cook until deep golden brown and crispy, turning once, 2 to 3 minutes per side.

7. Transfer to the prepared wire rack to drain. Repeat with the remaining pickles, letting the oil return to 360°F and topping up as needed before each batch.

8. Eat hot with ranch dressing.

LOADED FRIED OKRA
with Bacon and Juke Joint Ranch Dressing

This okra's motto is go big or go home, y'all. I use the biggest fresh okra when I make mine. Soakin' 'em first in the buttermilk is gonna take that sliminess outta 'em and make 'em golden brown and crispy when they're fried up. Use the prettiest, largest okra you can find in season for making these. Now, if you are in the South, you can find breaded okra in the frozen food section of the grocery store. That's also OK to use for this recipe . . . all you would need to do is follow the directions on the package and then add the same toppings. It's usually pretty good! So if you can grab that, do it!

If you like your ranch with a bite for dipping your okra, then give my Juke Joint Ranch Dressing (page 202) a couple hard shakes of your favorite hot sauce. That'll wake you up!

MAKES 2 TO 4 SERVINGS

1 pound fresh okra, tops and bottoms trimmed and cut into pieces

1 quart buttermilk

Canola or vegetable oil, for frying

About 2 cups Homemade Fish Fry (page 201), Juke Joint Fish Fry, or whatever Louisiana-style fish fry you've got in your neck of the woods

1 tablespoon House Seasoning Blend (page 200) or Juke Joint Seasoning

8 slices cooked bacon, or more if you want

Juke Joint Ranch Dressing (page 202)

1. Place the okra in a large bowl and cover with the buttermilk. Let sit at room temperature for up to an hour.

2. Place a wire rack inside a large baking sheet and set it next to the stovetop.

3. Add enough oil to come halfway up the sides of a large, heavy pot or deep-fat fryer and heat it to 350°F over medium-high heat.

4. Combine the fish fry and seasoning in a large bowl. Drop in the okra. No need to drain it first, just drop it in there.

5. Working in batches, give the okra a little shake to remove any excess and then carefully lay 'em out in the hot oil. Don't overcrowd that pot or they won't turn out sopped up! Cook, turning with a slotted spoon or tongs, until they're golden brown on all sides. When they float to the top, after 2 to 3 minutes, take 'em out and put them on the wire rack to drain. And if they bust out their seams like I do sometimes in my jeans, that's OK, too; they still gonna taste good.

6. Let the oil return to 350°F and then get back in there and finish cookin' up all the rest.

7. To serve, load up these babies on a big plate and crumble the bacon over the top. Put a big bowl of ranch on the side for dippin' and you're set!

PASTA SALAD

This is a traditional pasta salad that every Black southerner makes for every event: women's day at church, baby showers, family cookouts . . . you name it! You'll even find it at the juke joints for private functions. It's so danged delicious and easy to make! Oh—and I leave the skin on my cucumbers 'cuz I like the pop of color, but I do remove the seeds. Three-color, spiral-shaped pasta is most popular for this salad. You can use bow ties or other shapes, but you won't be an honorary southerner.

MAKES 6 TO 8 SERVINGS

One 16-ounce box tricolor spiral-shaped or bow tie pasta

2 medium cucumbers, halved lengthwise, seeded, and finely diced

3 large Roma tomatoes, finely diced

1½ cups Italian dressing, or more if you want (use your favorite brand)

1 cup Juke Joint Ranch Dressing (page 202)

2 good handfuls (about 2 cups) grated Parmesan, crumbled feta or goat cheese if you wanna be bougie, plus more for sprinkling

Salt and pepper to taste

I. Boil the pasta until tender according to the package instructions.

2. Drain well in a colander and let cool completely—don't add anything. If you do, the veggies won't stay crisp and fresh and the pasta is going to just vacuum up the dressing— and, hunny, you will be pouring dressing for days at a time trying to get it sopped up like you want it! The best thing to do is just simply wait for it to cool down, to avoid the trouble of folks complaining about a dry pasta salad. Promise!

3. Once the pasta has cooled completely, place it in a large bowl with the cucumbers,

tomatoes, Italian dressing, ranch dressing, Parmesan, and salt and pepper. Toss well.

4. Now is the time to adjust the seasonings. Taste the salad, and if you want more dressing, add it! Once the salad is like you like it, sprinkle a little bit more Parmesan on top. Now, here's the deal: you can eat this right away, but it's just better when it's cold, so I'll tell you to refrigerate it for 1 hour.

5. Store any leftovers tightly covered and refrigerated. This is perfect for snacking on during the week. (I mean, who the hell doesn't like to snack on pasta?)

SEAFOOD PIZZA

This pizza is so easy to make. It's perfect for brunch, dinner, or game night and only takes about 30 minutes, which is a plus for me. I like to parbake my dough for this pizza, since the sauce is cooked separately and seafood doesn't take long to cook. This way, the crust gets crispy, but the protein doesn't get overcooked.

MAKES ABOUT 4 SERVINGS

One 13.8-ounce can store-bought pizza dough
5 tablespoons salted butter
2 tablespoons Italian seasoning
2 cups heavy cream
1 tablespoon seafood seasoning

1 tablespoon garlic powder
1 teaspoon sazón (optional)
1 teaspoon kosher salt
1 teaspoon ground black pepper
1 tablespoon fresh lemon juice

1½ cups grated mozzarella
½ pound medium shrimp, peeled and deveined
½ cup crabmeat
½ cup grated white cheddar

I. Preheat the oven to 500°F.

2. Spread the dough in a large cast-iron pizza pan or on a baking sheet, following the directions on the package. Melt 3 tablespoons of the butter.

3. Brush the dough with melted butter and sprinkle with 1 tablespoon of the Italian seasoning. Reserve some of the melted butter for the finished pizza. Bake for about 8 minutes.

4. Meanwhile, start the sauce. Melt the remaining 2 tablespoons butter in a medium saucepan, then add the cream. Bring to a boil. Reduce the heat and simmer until slightly thickened, 5 to 6 minutes. Remove from the heat.

5. Stir in the seafood seasoning, garlic powder, sazón (if using), salt, pepper, and lemon juice.

Taste and adjust the flavor if you need to, adding more salt, lemon juice, or whatever you feel is missing.

6. Remove the pizza dough from the oven and let cool for about 2 minutes. It will seem slightly inflated but will deflate as it cools a bit.

7. Spread the sauce over the crust, then sprinkle 1 cup of the mozzarella on top. Add the shrimp and crabmeat and top with the remaining mozzarella and the cheddar.

8. Bake for another 10 to 12 minutes, until the top is slightly golden brown.

9. Remove from the oven and brush the edges with the reserved melted butter.

10. Serve HOT and ready!

Party
MEATBALLS

When I was growing up, if there was an event or party, these meatballs were always served—just like the Caramelized French Onion Dip (page 66). In hindsight, I know that the ones I loved back then were store-bought meatballs with bottled BBQ sauce!

But here's the thing, you gotta get the right meatballs and the right sauce. That's why we're making these with my Juke Joint Whiskey BBQ Sauce—although you can use a bottled sauce. It's so funny how something so simple can turn out so wrong if not done right. Every big club store and supermarket has frozen meatballs in big bags. They're fully cooked; you just need to heat them up and sop 'em up with sauce. I'm probably gonna get in trouble with my community for sharing this recipe and the secret to great party meatballs, but I'm sure I'll be forgiven over time!

MAKES ABOUT 12 DOZEN BITES

One 6-pound bag frozen fully cooked Italian-style beef meatballs

Juke Joint Whiskey BBQ Sauce (page 204) or two 18-ounce bottles BBQ sauce

1 cup honey

I. Preheat the oven to 350°F. Spray a large baking dish (or two smaller baking pans) with cooking spray.

2. Place the meatballs—still frozen—in the prepared dish.

3. Pour the sauce and honey all over the top. Give it a stir to coat everything. Cover tightly with foil and bake for 30 minutes. Uncover and continue baking until bubbly, caramelized, and smellin' so good, about 20 more minutes.

4. Spoon the meatballs into a nice serving platter or bowl and serve hot with toothpicks or little forks and lotsa cocktail napkins. Watch out—everybody gonna go crazy!

Juke Joint
CHARCUTERIE PLATTER

Usually on a charcuterie platter you get somethin' bougie, like Italian meat, jams, figs, and Spanish olives. The longer I live in LA, the more bougie my ass gets . . . I love a good charcuterie platter! But when I was growing up, we got souse meat—ain't no prosciutto on the Westside—from the Piggly Wiggly. It's like hog's head cheese, and we ate it with saltines . . . you talk about DIVINE!

What I've included for you here are some flavorful pickles you can make for a little juke joint platter at home. Pile these peppers up on a big platter with some sliced meats from the store, a bunch of different cheeses and crackers, grapes . . . hell, you know what to do! And add some Party Meatballs (page 86) and BBQ Pulled Pork (page 26) while you're add it. Oh! And wine! Open some wine!

PICKLED EGGS

Pickled eggs are a favorite of mine. Ain't a barroom in the South that doesn't have a jar of reddish pickled eggs on the bar. My daddy use to sell them in his juke joint for fifty cents each. I remember taking my first bite and thinking, "What the hell is this?," but then I couldn't stop eating it! The yolk is the best part if ya ask me, especially if you sprinkle a little extra salt on it. I like them sliced on top of a salad.

My uncle Walter is the one who taught me to add garlic powder to my pickles. Try it, y'all—life changing. Puckery, melt-in-ya-mouth hard-boiled eggs! Mmm, mmm, mmm!

MAKES 8 TO 10

8 to 10 large eggs, hard-boiled (see page 65), peeled and left whole

1 cup apple cider vinegar

1½ cups distilled white vinegar

3 tablespoons sugar

2 tablespoons garlic powder

1 tablespoon kosher salt

1 tablespoon pickling spice

1 teaspoon red food coloring (optional; if you wanna keep them white, don't add it)

I. Put the eggs into a sterilized jar.

2. Combine 1 cup water, the vinegars, sugar, garlic powder, salt, pickling spice, and food coloring (if using) in a medium saucepan. Bring the mixture to a boil, stirring to dissolve the sugar and salt.

3. Remove from the heat and let cool slightly, about 2 minutes. Pour the hot liquid over the eggs to cover by ½ inch. Tap the jar to release any air pockets and add more liquid as needed.

4. Let cool to room temperature and then close tightly with the lid.

5. Refrigerate for at least 4 days before eating. These will keep in the fridge for up to 2 months.

Note You'll need one half-gallon (64-ounce) wide-mouth Mason jar, or two 1-quart (32-ounce) wide-mouth Mason jars, sterilized (see page 95).

Somethin' to Snack On

PICKLED PEPPERS

Tangy, spicy, and downright delicious, pickled peppers are great with just about anything. I pickle my peppers whole and love to eat 'em that way with the Spatchcocked Whole Fried Chicken (page 113). These are also so tasty cut up in Pot Liquor Greens (page 148), and I add them to my salads and tacos. The possibilities are endless, y'all. Store these in the fridge for up to 2 months.

MAKES 1 QUART

1 pound fresh jalapeño peppers, stemmed

1 cup distilled white vinegar
2 tablespoons kosher salt

1 tablespoon pickling spice
2 tablespoons sugar

I. Pack the peppers into a sterilized jar and let 'em hang out a little while you make the pickling liquid.

2. Combine 1 cup water, the vinegar, salt, pickling spice, and sugar in a medium saucepan. Bring the mixture to a boil, stirring to dissolve the sugar and salt.

3. Remove from the heat and let cool, about 10 minutes. Pour the liquid over the peppers to cover by ½ inch. Tap the jar to release any air pockets and add more liquid as needed.

4. Let cool to room temperature and then close tightly with the lid.

5. Refrigerate for at least 2 days before eating. These will keep in the fridge for up to 2 months.

> **Note** You'll need a 1-quart (32-ounce) wide-mouth Mason jar, sterilized (see page 95).

PICKLED SAUSAGES

Everybody's got their favorite smoked sausage. I think the best are from Conecuh or Roger Wood—but I'm biased, it's what we ate growin' up! Use what's good near you, and Hillshire Farm will do fine. And because you're using smoked sausage—which is cured or precooked—in this recipe, you don't need to cook your sausage.

Of all pickles, pickled sausage has always been one of my favorite snacks. In Alabama I could find it everywhere, even at the ice cream trucks, but when I moved to LA and could no longer get it, I found it online and had it shipped to me instead! Finally, I decided to make my own, and this recipe might just make you addicted, too.

Just be sure to grab a cold sparkling drank to enjoy (these are REALLY great with a peach wine cooler or the Jack & Pepsi Slushies on page 2) and tell me this don't feel like a southern hot summer day, walking down the street to meet your friend to play.

MAKES 2 POUNDS

2 pounds smoked sausage, cut into 2- to 3-inch pieces
1½ cups distilled white vinegar
1 cup apple cider vinegar

2 tablespoons sugar
1 tablespoon pickling spice
1 tablespoon garlic powder

1 tablespoon onion powder
1 teaspoon kosher salt
1 teaspoon red food coloring

1. Place the sausages in a sterilized jar.

2. Combine 1 cup water, the vinegars, sugar, pickling spice, garlic powder, onion powder, salt, and food coloring in a medium saucepan. Bring the mixture to a boil, stirring to dissolve the sugar and salt.

3. Remove from the heat and let cool slightly, about 2 minutes. Pour the hot liquid over the sausages to cover by ½ inch. Tap the jar to release any air pockets and add more liquid as needed.

4. Let cool to room temperature and then close tightly with the lid.

5. Refrigerate for at least a week before eating. These will keep in the fridge for up to 2 months.

Note You'll need one half-gallon (64-ounce) wide-mouth Mason jar, or two 1-quart (32-ounce) wide-mouth Mason jars, sterilized (see page 95).

QUICK PICKLING TIPS

In the South, we pickle just about everything, hunny. Pickled pigs' feet, pickled pigs' ears, pickled eggs, pickled vegetables, even pickled fruit!

All my pickling recipes in this chapter are for "quick" pickles. This means these pickles are refrigerator pickled, not hot packed (or canned). They *must be kept in the refrigerator* after they're placed in the jars with their pickling liquid. Don't leave these out at room temperature!

- Use kosher salt for pickling; it'll keep your pickled peppers and other veggies crisper than regular table salt.

- You can buy pickling spice at the supermarket. Or you can make your own spice blend to suit your tastes, with whole or coarse-ground black pepper, cloves, cinnamon, ginger . . . you name it!

- Sterilize your jars and lids *before* packing them with your pickling ingredients. All that means, y'all, is put 'em in a big pot of boiling water to cover and let them boil for 10 minutes. Carefully remove with tongs, dump out the water, and let cool before filling. Easy!

- Because these pickles are stored in the fridge, you should eat them within 2 months. The ones you buy in the store have been hot packed or canned and so can be kept longer.

- Quick pickles will continue to develop flavors once you've packed and refrigerated them. They're best when they've cured for about 2 weeks. But I like to eat them as soon as 3 days in. They are still great if you're like me and can't wait.

THE MAIN THANG

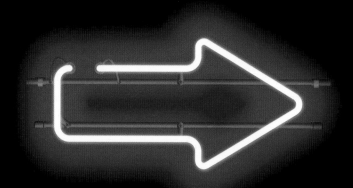

Like my daddy always said, you gotta keep the main thang.

We got the dranks, somethin' to snack on, and now we got the meals that will have people looking for you in the daytime with a flashlight. These here are the bangers . . . or as my mama would say, "So now we cookin' with gas."

These are the meals I make for my folk, and, hunny, let me tell you, when they eat these dishes, you can sell them for a penny and get change . . . they get so weak in the knees! Anyway, let's get into it!

SOUTHERN FRIED FISH
with Homemade Fish Fry and Juke Joint Tartar Sauce

Where I grew up, you get your grits with fried fish, not shrimp, so try this with my Savory Cheese Grits (page 29). That's also one of those Alabama things you have to eat on New Year's Eve. And before you start on your fish, you gotta make some of my good Homemade Fish Fry (page 201) so yours'll be real sopped up.

Load this up onto a southern-style seafood platter with Fried Scallops (page 107), Fried Dill Pickle Spears (page 75), and Ole Skool Mac 'n' Cheese (page 142), and make a mess of Loaded Fried Okra (page 76) while the oil is still hot! Be sure to mix up some Juke Joint Tartar Sauce (page 98) while you're at it. Or you do you and grab what you like.

MAKES 4 SERVINGS

Canola or vegetable oil, for frying

2 to 3 pounds fresh farm-raised catfish, or whatever fish variety you wanna use, patted dry with paper towels (if all you can get is frozen, thaw safely in the fridge overnight)

1 cup yellow mustard

1 tablespoon Old Bay Seasoning

Homemade Fish Fry (page 201), Juke Joint Fish Fry, or whatever Louisiana-style fish fry you've got in your neck of the woods

Juke Joint Tartar Sauce (page 203), or store-bought

I. Place a wire rack inside a large sheet pan and set it next to the stove so it's all ready for when the fish comes out of the oil.

2. Add enough oil to come about 2 inches up the sides of a large cast-iron skillet or Dutch oven and heat it to 375°F over medium-high heat. (You know we Black people be using that cast iron, hunny, 'cuz it holds the heat very, very well and helps your food cook evenly.)

3. Spread out the fish on a work surface or a couple plates and coat both sides with the mustard. (You won't taste the mustard! It just ensures the fish stays nice and tender and helps the fish fry to stick to it, all up inside the crevices and everything, like you want!)

4. Season the fillets on both sides with the Old Bay. This is insurance to give it extra flava; I don't wanna put the Old Bay in the fish fry directly 'cuz sometimes that'll make it a little bitter, but I do like to add it to my fish before cookin' it.

5. One at a time, place a fish fillet in the fish fry, and with your hands, press that fish fry all up in there and get it covered real good, turning to

coat it on both sides and up in the edges. Shake off the excess back into the bowl.

6. Add 2 fish fillets to the hot oil, layin' 'em down away from you so you don't get spattered. And don't overcrowd that pan—that'll make your fish soggy! Cook 'em on both sides till they're all crispy and crunchy, 3 to 5 minutes per side, depending on how thick your fillets are. And you know it's doin' it's stuff, 'cuz that hot oil sounds like food rain, it's so calming. Transfer the cooked fish to the wire rack to drain and let the oil come back up to 375°F (this takes about 2 minutes or so).

7. Repeat with the remaining fish, coating and frying until they're flaky and crispy. Y'all know what I'm talkin' about! Serve hot with tartar sauce.

Fish Fry Sandwich

Across the South, fish fry sandwiches can be found on just about every corner and in little spots throughout the hood. My mama and them were always frying fish back in the day for the church or social savings club (see page 66) to make money.

When you order your sandwich, you gotta ask for it to be "all the way," which means fried fish on sliced soft white bread with mustard, ketchup, and hot sauce. They'll also sprinkle a little black pepper on there if you want 'em to. There's no tartar sauce or buns or pickles—it's just fried fish at its best. And my Southern Fried Fish with Homemade Fish Fry recipe (page 98) is the right way to cook it.

At little places like my daddy's Haywood's Place, Green Acres, Lily Pearl's, the Handsome Brutes, Wellington's Bistro, and others, you'd order fish fry sandwiches and hang out at the bar. At Mama & Sons, another great hole-in-the-wall, they had the best fried chicken and Sunday buffet. I'd go there every Sunday night to sing the blues. Yes, chile, I can sing a tune or two . . . Hell, I use to sing blues and do a dinner party in the same night.

If you make your fish sandwich *all the way* like this, you will never want Chilean sea bass again.

MAKES 1 SANDWICH

2 slices Sunbeam bread, or other soft white bread

1 catfish fillet, prepared following the instructions on page 99

Yellow mustard

Ketchup

Hot sauce

Ground black pepper

1. Lay the bread on a plate.

2. Put that hot fish right outta the skillet and place it on wire rack or a plate lined with a paper towel to drain the grease off the fish, then place the fish on a slice of bread and dress it up the way you like with mustard and ketchup. Sprinkle on some hot sauce and a shake or two of black pepper, then top with the other slice of bread.

3. Now take a bite. It's gonna be soooooo good the way that bread's gonna stick to the roof of your mouth and the crust on the fish crunches! That's a bite of the South right there.

FRIED SCALLOPS
with Juke Joint Tartar Sauce

I'm always so surprised when folks tell me they've never had fried scallops! Well, hunny, where I'm from, if you fry it, we'll try it! Most folks would sear these suckers and finish 'em with a pretty bland sauce and fresh cracked pepper or somethin' on top. But today, we're throwin' these into a deep-frying Jacuzzi and letting the oil do the work, hunny.

Unless you live by the water, your scallops are frozen, baby. And I know these are expensive, so get however many you can afford. Save some money and buy the frozen ones at your Costco or wherever. They freeze 'em on the boat right after they're caught, so the freshness is locked in. Thaw in the fridge when you're ready to use 'em.

On Friday nights, my dad would take us to a little place called Bryant's Seafood. It was a small shack, hunny! If you turned around once in it, you'd be outdoors. But the best things come in small packages. At Bryant's, the seafood was served up in a little plastic basket, and you had a choice of a "pick two" or "pick three" for your basket. My pick three was fried fish, shrimp, and scallops.

Like I do with my Southern Fried Fish (page 98), I lightly coat the raw scallops on both sides in yellow mustard; this helps the fish fry stick to them and promotes browning.

MAKES 2 TO 4 SERVINGS, DEPENDIN' ON WHAT'S IN YOUR SEAFOOD BASKET

Canola or vegetable oil, for frying

1 pound large sea scallops (10 to 20 per pound), rinsed under cold running water and patted dry

3 tablespoons yellow mustard

2 cups Homemade Fish Fry (page 201), Juke Joint Fish Fry, or whatever Louisiana-style fish fry you've got in your neck of the woods

Juke Joint Tartar Sauce (page 203)

1. Place a wire rack inside a large baking sheet and set it next to the stovetop.

2. Add enough oil to come halfway up the sides of a large, heavy pot or deep-fat fryer and heat it to 350°F over medium-high heat. (You can also shallow fry these in a large cast-iron skillet or heavy pan. Just use less oil.)

3. Place the scallops and mustard in a large bowl, and gently rub to evenly coat.

4. Put the fish fry in a paper bag or large freezer bag and add the scallops, 4 or 5 at a time. Seal the bag and shake lightly to coat.

5. Carefully add the scallops to the hot oil in batches and cook, turning once with a slotted spoon or tongs, until they're cooked through, golden brown, and start floating to the top, 3 to 5 minutes, depending on the size.

6. Take 'em out with a slotted spoon and put on the wire rack to drain. Serve hot with tartar sauce.

Fried & Laid to the Side
TIPS FOR SOPPED-UP FRIED FOOD

Now we're gonna do a lil fryin'—open up the windows!

When it comes to frying, we've got a couple of rules. Listen, this is not the time to bring out your air fryer. I'm also still confused on how air can "fry" something, but I digress . . .

Rule #1: You fry it, I'll try it! And remember, I'm a cook, not your doctor, but in my opinion, there are no bad foods . . . just bad relationships with food. Every now and again, you just need something crispy.

Rule #2: You need to wear the proper attire. Now is not the time to be cute. You get a pass for lookin' tore up from the floor up, because this is serious business! Grab your favorite house dress, the most comfortable, raggedy one you got, or a tore-up T-shirt and shorts, and put on your flip-flops or Jesus sandals because toes being out is a must when fryin'. And for all my ladies, don't forget your gold anklet. I promise you, anything you make while wearing it is gonna be Sopped Up!

Ready?

This is not the time to sous vide or sear. Ain't nobody trying to be Gordon Ramsay. I always like to start with a standard temperature when fryin' to make sure we're being safe. For me, 350° to 375°F is about right.

Most people who are familiar with fryin' test the oil by sprinkling a li'l bit of flour or a drop of batter into the grease; if it bubbles, the temp is right and you're ready to go. But a thermometer or a deep-fat fryer with automatic temperature control is a good way to go for all you out there who are still workin' on figuring it out. It's OK, I got you. We are in this thing together.

When you slide your food into that hot grease, you have to be super careful. Take your time. Gently slide whatever you're fryin' into the hot oil, and make sure you slide it *AWAY from you* into the pan or you're gonna be lookin' like Fire Marshall Bill. And ain't nobody got time for that!

Your food should start bubbling when it hits the oil. Otherwise, instead of it being golden brown and crisp to perfection, it's gonna look like my daddy's tired Jheri curl, and then you're gonna really have people talkin'—just not in a good way.

Remember, never overcrowd your pan. Just a little PSA from the SCC (Sopped-Up Community Church): when you're fryin', you need to social distance your food. Or it's gonna steam and not fry.

How Do You Know It's Done?

Hunny, that's simple: consider it a food resurrection! Whatever you're fryin' should float to the top of the oil and be melanated—that's beautiful brown—on all sides.

And when you take that food out of the fryin' oil, it should be steamin' like a woman on the Maury Povich show.

What Else?

Don't put your just-fried food on paper towels to drain! That may be ole skool, but it'll make your food sweat and it'll get all soggy. And you don't want that after all that hot oil Jacuzzi love you just gave it!

I learned from Emeril, watchin' the Food Network when I was comin' up, to put my fried food straight away on a wire rack set inside a baking sheet. The wire rack lets the air circulate and keeps the food crispy, and the baking catches the grease. One and done!

I don't add extra salt or seasoning when the food comes out of the oil, 'cuz it's already sopped up from the seasoning I gave it first. If you're using my Homemade Fish Fry (page 201) or any of my recipes here, you probably won't need to add more salt, but I can't speak for other brands.

Just taste it when it's cooled down a little and take it from there.

Spatchcocked
WHOLE FRIED CHICKEN

Hunny, trust me, you got to have your chicken spatchcocked for this to work. You make those Yeasted Drop Biscuits with Butta (page 35) and Pickled Peppers (page 92), and you got a Church's Chicken right in your house! And maybe some of that Ole Skool Mac 'n' Cheese (page 142) or Cheesy Broccoli & Rice Casserole (page 159).

Now, there are two ways you can make this: with or without breading. We're makin' the one with breading here; you can figure out the nekkid one on your own, just not usin' the batter, chile! But one thing that's a must any way you make fried chicken: you gotta toss your chicken with the House Seasoning Blend on page 200 (or Juke Joint Seasoning) both before *and* after the bird gets its hot oil Jacuzzi treatment!

OK, y'all . . . Now it's time to get down like James Brown, 'cuz this recipe is so doggone good! The chicken is juicy, tender, crispy, and, believe it or not, not that hard to make. (I know, right?) We are gonna remove the backbone so the bird lays flat because it cuts the cooking time in half and allows the chicken to cook properly. This is a fo' sho' showstopper. OK, I've talked too much. Lemme teach you how to make it—and this one needs a few extra tips.

Preppin' Your Bird

Be sure to pluck any remaining feathers that may be on the chicken. (You don't want the chicken to fly away; it has already flown, hunny.) Don't trim any excess fat or skin; it turns into the best crispy bits and cracklin' when you fry it.

Especially when frying, you never want to cook protein right out of the pack. After you rinse the chicken well under cold running water—and clean out the inside, too—let it sit on a big plate out on the counter for 30 to 45 minutes. This helps keep the meat from drying out when you cook it, and it also helps it cook evenly. Don't skip this step! If you try to use cold-outta-the-fridge chicken, the outside can cook faster than the inside, leaving you with sad, disappointing meat.

I also like to use sturdy kitchen scissors, an underutilized tool, instead of a knife to cut out the backbone. (Stop cutting your lace-front wigs with your sharp kitchen shears, girl. Save them for the kitchen!)

Then, after one final rinse in cold water, pat the chicken dry all over with paper towels (this is important, because you want to remove the excess moisture). OK, we're ready. Now if you need to read this again, do just that. Have no shame in your game.

Seasonin' a.k.a. My Juke Joint Seasoning (or House Seasoning Blend I've Given You in This Book)

I know there is a lot of seasoning in this recipe. Hunny, don't be scared: seasoning is not your enemy, it is a friend till the end. You've got a whole chicken that needs to be sopped up and seasoned.

And now is the time to give your chicken a name. My mama always said that if you name your plants and treat them right, they are gonna grow, so we're gonna do the same with our chickens. Depending on what I'm feelin', I change up the names, and today I'm feelin' sassy, so this hen is Miss Peaches.

Pancake Mix

Yup, you saw that right. We are using pancake mix in the batter. This is going to allow the skin to get nice and crispy and remove an extra step of breading. But don't worry, the fried coating will not be sweet at all. We ain't makin' chicken cobbler, hunny!

You can use this same batter with almost anything you're frying—pork chops, chicken wings, veggies (broccoli, green beans). Just don't use it on Southern Fried Fish (page 98); we want something with a li'l cornmeal in there. (If you want something more like fish and chips, like the Brits do with cod, this would be OK.)

One 4- to 5-pound whole chicken

1 cup or so House Seasoning Blend (page 200) or Juke Joint Seasoning

Canola or vegetable oil, for frying

3 cups buttermilk pancake mix, whichever one you like

3 cups self-rising flour

Yeasted Drop Biscuits with Butta (page 35), for serving

Pickled Peppers (page 92), for serving

1. Pluck off any bits of feathers, if there are any, then rinse the chicken under cold running water and allow it to sit out on the counter at room temperature for 30 to 45 minutes. Wash out your sink real good with a soapy solution and paper towels to get it safely sanitized all over again when you done.

2. Remove the tailbone by laying the chicken, breast side down, on the cutting board. Now use your kitchen scissors to cut along each side of the backbone, all the way from the tailbone to the top where the neck was, and pull it out. (And save that backbone for stock or to season your rice. Stick it in a plastic zip-top bag in the freezer till you wanna use it.)

3. Rinse the inside of the chicken well to remove any blood and grit, and put Miss Peaches, or whateva you callin' your chicken, on a large plate lined with paper towels. Pat her dry all over with paper towels to remove the excess moisture. Be sure to properly sanitize your area and sink!

4. Now, I want you to take ½ cup of the seasoning and sprinkle it over the chicken. Be sure to get it in all the creases of Miss Peaches, both sides, too, so use your hands. You want to rub this chicken just like you would want

someone to rub you at night, OK? If the chicken still looks like it ain't quite sopped up and needs more seasoning, add a li'l more. Don't be scared, hunny, it's already dead—it can't hurt you. After you've done that, push it to the side to sit for a minute while you get everything else ready. And wash your hands real good.

5. Line a large baking sheet with paper towels and place a wire rack inside. Set it next to the stovetop for drainin' that chicken when it's done.

6. Fill a large, heavy pot, a deep Dutch oven—cast iron if you got it—or a large deep-fat fryer (remove the basket) with enough oil to come halfway up the sides (you want a good 6 inches of oil). Heat the oil to 325°F over medium heat until it glistens, 5 to 7 minutes if you've got a big, wide Dutch oven, maybe a li'l bit longer if you're using more of a collard greens pot. Check the oil temperature with a candy or deep-fat thermometer, if you have one.

7. While the oil heats, combine your pancake mix and 1½ cups of water in a large bowl and mix with a fork until it's smooth as a baby's bottom (we're not makin' pancakes).

8. In a second large bowl, whisk together the self-rising flour and the remaining ½ cup seasoning.

recipe continues

9. Now it's time to fry! Gently lay the chicken in the pancake mix, using your hands to cover Miss Peaches all over with the mix. Now add her to the bowl with the seasoned flour and toss her in it real well, and then shake her a li'l bit to get the excess flour off.

10. Gently place the coated chicken into your pot or deep fryer and fry until browned on the underside, 15 minutes. Use tongs to *carefully* lift up Miss Peaches and flip her over to brown on the other side. Cook until she floats to the top of the oil, 15 to 20 minutes longer, depending on the size of your bird. If you aren't sure about whether she's good and cooked, insert an instant-read thermometer in the thickest part of her big ole juicy thigh. It should read 165°F when she's done.

11. Use your tongs to transfer Miss Peaches to the prepared rack. Let her cool down for a few minutes, maybe 10 at most (enough time to get another drank), and serve her while she's HOT, hunny, with those biscuits and pickled jalapeños on the side.

Country-Style Chicken Tacos

If you've got any leftover fried chicken (or that Chicken Butta Chicken, page 119), make these sopped-up chicken tacos and you've got the best easy weeknight supper. These tacos are a reason to make extra fried chicken, I swear!

Or, if you want to make a bunch of these, then use the method for boilin' your chicken, like in the Club Meetin' Chicken Salad (page 58). Cook up a whole chicken or breast, shred that meat, and you'll have enough for a chicken taco party to go with your Suburban Mom margaritas (page 13).

If you're more in the salad mood, then pile all these ingredients together in a bowl, toss with the dressing, and serve with a big bowl of tortilla chips on the side.

MAKES HOWEVER MANY SERVINGS YOU'VE GOT LEFTOVERS FOR!

Flour or corn tortillas, whichever you like best

Leftover Spatchcocked Whole Fried Chicken (page 113), pulled off the bone and shredded into bite-size pieces

Shredded lettuce or cabbage

Thinly sliced yellow onions

Chopped fresh tomatoes

Juke Joint Ranch Dressing (page 202)

Hot sauce, if you're spicy minded

1. This here recipe is super easy—just make it any way you like it!

2. To make soft tacos, place your tortillas between paper towels on a plate and microwave on high for about 10 seconds.

3. Pile 'em high with shredded chicken and top with lettuce, onions, and tomatoes. Drizzle 'em real good with ranch dressing and some hot sauce (if you want), then serve 'em up!

♦

Danni's Juke Joint Comfort Food

Chicken Butta
CHICKEN

I use a big cast-iron skillet when I'm roasting chicken because it helps the skin caramelize and get nice and crispy on the bottom. This whole chicken is bathed first in chicken-flavored butta, roasted in the oven, and then finished with more butta! I heard the French folks like to bathe food in butta, so I guess we can say, "Oui, oui!" Hunny, grab your beret and let's get it started!

MAKES 2 TO 4 SERVINGS

One 3- to 4-pound chicken, at room temperature, patted dry and spatchcocked (see page 113)

1 cup (2 sticks) salted butta, at room temperature

2 tablespoons chicken-flavored bouillon powder

2 tablespoons dried parsley

2 tablespoons garlic powder

2 teaspoons kosher salt

2 teaspoons paprika

1 teaspoon ground black pepper

1 lemon, cut in half

1. Preheat the oven to 375°F.

2. Place the chicken in a 12-inch cast-iron skillet or large baking dish.

3. Now we wanna make our butta. Super simple. Combine the softened butta, bouillon, parsley, garlic powder, salt, paprika, and pepper in a medium bowl and mix well with a fork into a smooth paste. You can taste the butta before adding it to the chicken and adjust the seasoning if it needs it. Just take a little taste; it ain't gonna hurt you.

4. Rub half the butta all over the chicken and even underneath the skin . . . we gotta get it sopped up! It's gonna seem a little gross, but, hunny, you just wait—good things come from ugly beginnings sometimes.

5. Wash your hands, tent the pan with foil, and bake until the chicken is starting to get tender, 45 minutes to 1 hour. Remove the foil and increase the temperature to 450°F. Continue baking until the chicken is cooked through, the juices run clear, and the skin is crispy and golden

recipe continues

brown, about 20 minutes. Remove from the oven and place the pan on top of the stove.

6. Add the remaining chicken-flavored butta to the pan while it's still good 'n' hot. The butter should sizzle and melt immediately, just like me when I see a good-looking man who smells good—hunny, talk about weak in the knees. But lemme focus . . . back to the chicken! Grab a large spoon, and baste the chicken with the melted chicken butta, and get it nice and sopped up in there.

7. Now, let the chicken rest about 20 minutes before you cut into it. We want those juices to stay in, not run out the door like someone is chasing them for money.

8. Cut the chicken into pieces as desired, then give them a squeeze of fresh lemon juice and serve with Sour Cream & Onion Mashed Potatoes (page 161), Basic Rice (page 210), or Cheesy Broccoli & Rice Casserole with Potato Chip Topping (page 159). And that's a winner-winner chicken dinner!

SOPPED-UP CHICKEN BASICS

Here's what you need to do to start makin' your chicken sopped up.

1. Let the chicken sit out a bit to come to almost room temp. You never want to cook any protein straight out of the pack. Always let it hang out on a plate before cooking for about 1 hour or so, because it keeps the meat from getting tough and dry. Wonder why your chicken is giving you cotton mouth? You're probably cooking it straight out of the pack . . . Don't do that anymore, OK?

2. I like to clean my chicken first. Yes. I'm Black and we like to clean our chicken, hunny. So, if you are like me, you probably already know how to do this step.

3. If you're not or don't know, then rinse that bird real good under cold running water, including the inside.

4. Once the chicken is cleaned, place it in a cookin' pan or on a big plate and pat dry with a couple paper towels. At this point be sure to clean and sanitize your sink and surfaces—anything that has been in contact with the raw chicken.

5. Then set that bird aside and get to makin' the recipe.

PS—Let whatever other proteins you're plannin' to cook come to room temperature also. You don't have to rinse them. Just let 'em sit there for a while.

The World's Best
DOUBLE CHEESEBURGER

This is my take on what I think is the world's greatest double cheeseburger, which is from Milo's in Birmingham, Alabama (though they now have locations all over). What makes theirs so special? Everything! It's the way they char both sides of the bun, flatten their patties and cook 'em on a big flat-top griddle, and the way the cheese gets all melted into the meat. They don't use lettuce or tomatoes, and thank the Lord, no mayonnaise—just a secret Milo's sauce that is to die for! I took a stab at it here, but you can use my Juke Joint Whiskey BBQ Sauce (page 204), if you'd prefer.

This recipe makes one double cheeseburger—that's what my daddy loved and it's just right for me. You can double this recipe or ramp it up for however many people you're cookin' for. You'll have plenty of sauce—or if it's just you, save your extra sauce in the fridge for up to 1 week or in the freezer up to 1 month. Milo's serves their burgers with salted crinkle-cut French fries and sweet tea. Make a batch of my Juke Joint Spiked Tea (page 5) and a mess of fries, and you'll be set.

MAKES 1 DOUBLE CHEESEBURGER

1 cup ketchup

½ cup A.1. Original Sauce

Two 6-ounce beef patties, I like 80/20—you can use anything, just no ground turkey!

Kosher salt and ground black pepper to taste

1 tablespoon canola or vegetable oil

2 slices American cheese, if you want it authentic, but I like smoked Gouda

1 hamburger bun

2 tablespoons chunky-cut white or yellow onion

3 dill pickle slices

1. Whisk together the ketchup and A.1. in a small bowl and set aside. (Or serve this with my Juke Joint Whiskey BBQ Sauce on page 204 instead.)

2. Get a large cast-iron or other heavy skillet good and hot over medium heat.

3. Put some wax paper down on a large plate and flatten both patties. Season lightly with salt and pepper on both sides. And wash your hands!

4. Put the oil in the pan, add the meat, and cook until well seared, about 2 minutes. Flip with a spatula, place 1 slice of cheese on top of each patty, and cook until seared on the bottom, about 2 minutes.

5. Transfer the meat to a clean plate to rest. Place the bun straightaway into the fat in the hot pan and char, about 30 seconds per side.

6. Place the bun on the plate and slather the sauce on both sides. Stack the burgers and top with the onion and pickles. Eat right away with extra sauce on the side.

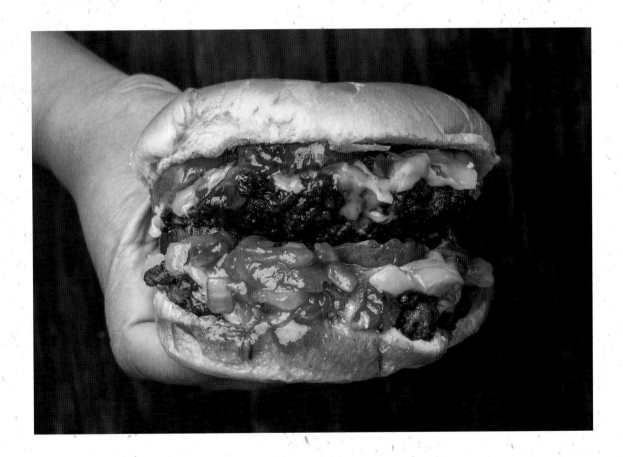

Juke Joint
CAJUN SPAGHETTI AND MEATBALLS

Miss Verna is an amazing family friend from Lafayette, Louisiana. Her son, Tyrone, is married to my cousin Kita. And in my family, if we like you, we all family now. So, we were all family, planning our joint family reunion together, and, hunny, it was *lit*! And that's when I tried this life-changing, tongue-smackin' spaghetti dish. I still call Kita to ask Verna to make this delicious pot of gold every time I'm about to see her.

Now, Miss Verna never gave me her recipe. But that's OK! I decided to make up my own sopped-up version and add a few things that I like. So, Miss Verna, this was inspired by you! I hope you like it.

Here's how I do mine at home: I make only eight meatballs from this recipe, 'cuz I like 'em big and juicy. You can make yours smaller if you like them better that way. Also, I prefer these roasted in a cast-iron skillet to get that crust on them. Just slide that cast iron into the oven like you would a baking pan. If you don't have cast iron, it's all good. Use any heavy, ovenproof pan you got.

If you don't eat beef, you can make the meatballs with ground turkey or chicken, or even chicken or turkey sausage taken out of the casings. I live in LA now, so I'm used to people eatin' skinny food. If you can't find real andouille, Hillshire Farm's andouille sausage is the next best thing. If you don't have a food scale, hunny, just cut one of those 13-ounce Hillshire Farm sausages in half.

Oh! And I ain't never tasted the difference between a red, green, yellow, or orange bell pepper. Just cook whatever kind you like best. But whatever you use, you're gonna want a lot of this sauce on your plate, it's that good.

Growing up, my mama put everything together in the pot and stirred it together—the meat sauce and the spaghetti. But I like to serve my pasta like the Italian restaurants do, with a big spoonful of sauce in the bowl first, and then I top it with spaghetti, more sauce, and a meatball. I sprinkle it with Parmesan and serve it good and hot!

Cajun spaghetti sauce

½ cup olive oil

½ cup chopped bell pepper (any color)

½ cup chopped yellow onion

3 tablespoons garlic powder

3 tablespoons onion powder

3 tablespoons tomato paste

2 tablespoons brown sugar

2 tablespoons Juke Joint Black Cajun Seasoning, or other Cajun seasoning blend

2 tablespoons Italian seasoning

1 tablespoon crushed red pepper

1 tablespoon kosher salt, or to taste

1 cup red wine, whatever you like best

Two 28-ounce cans crushed tomatoes and their juices

One 14-ounce can diced tomatoes and their juices

2 tablespoons beef-flavored bouillon powder

¼ cup (½ stick) salted butter

Andouille meatballs

2 slices sandwich bread, whatever kind you like

1½ cups whole milk

1 pound ground beef or sirloin

6 to 8 ounces andouille sausage, finely diced

1 large egg

½ cup chopped bell pepper (any color)

½ cup chopped yellow onion

3 tablespoons Italian seasoning

2 tablespoons garlic powder

2 tablespoons onion powder

2 tablespoons paprika

1 tablespoon Juke Joint Black Cajun Seasoning, or other Cajun seasoning blend

2 teaspoons beef-flavored bouillon powder

1 teaspoon ground black pepper

Two 16-ounce packages spaghetti, whatever brand you like best

1 cup grated Parmesan

1. To make the sauce, heat the oil in a large pot or Dutch oven over medium heat. Add the bell pepper and onion and cook until soft, about 3 minutes. Add the garlic and onion powders, tomato paste, brown sugar, Cajun and Italian seasonings, crushed red pepper, and salt and cook, stirring, until fragrant and the tomato paste starts to turn brown, about 1 minute.

2. Add the wine, stir well, and then add a little mo' if you've had a rough day. Cook until the wine is evaporated by half, about 2 minutes. Now add in the tomatoes. Add 3 cups water and the bouillon, stir well, and bring to a boil.

3. Reduce the heat to low and cook until the sauce is thick and juicy, like me, about 45 minutes, stirring occasionally to keep it from stickin' to the pot. Stir in the butter, remove from the heat, and cover to keep warm.

recipe continues

4. While the sauce is cooking, prepare the meatballs and cook your spaghetti in boiling water according to the package instructions. You don't wanna waste time and have to wait to eat, hunny!

5. Preheat the oven to 350°F. Lightly grease a cast-iron skillet, so you can get crusty sides and bottoms on your meatballs. (Or line a large baking pan with foil and spray with cooking spray.)

6. Tear the bread into small pieces and place in a large bowl. Add the milk and let soak until the milk is absorbed, about 5 minutes.

7. Add the beef, sausage, egg, bell pepper, onion, Italian seasoning, garlic and onion powders, paprika, Cajun seasoning, bouillon, and pepper and mix well by hand for 30 seconds, being careful not to overmix.

8. To form the meatballs, scoop the mixture, about a heaping ⅓ cup each, into the prepared skillet (or onto the baking sheet) and bake until cooked through and browned on all sides, 20 to 22 minutes.

9. Using a spoon, transfer the meatballs to the tomato sauce for a little meet 'n' greet. Stir, and let 'em rub elbows for 5 minutes.

10. To serve, place sauce into each pasta bowl or large plate. Add a heapin' helpin' of spaghetti, top with more sauce, and then place a meatball on top and sprinkle with the Parmesan.

SUNDAY POT ROAST
with Cognac Gravy

As I've told you before (back on page 123), room temperature meat cooks better than cold. Promise! I never cook meat cold outta the pack, 'cuz that's the sure way to get dry, tough meat.

For this recipe, cube your meat before you let it come to room temperature. It's also important to cook your meat in batches so it browns and doesn't steam while cooking.

And hey now, if you're doin' this in a slow cooker, then just throw everything in there and cook it on low for 8 hours. This pot roast is extra amazing served over Savory Cheese Grits (page 29).

MAKES 4 TO 6 SERVINGS

2½ pounds boneless beef chuck roast or chuck tender roast, cut into 2-inch cubes

3 tablespoons House Seasoning Blend (page 200) or Juke Joint Seasoning

½ cup canola or vegetable oil

1 large yellow onion, thinly sliced

¼ cup beef-flavored bouillon powder

2 tablespoons dried thyme

2½ cups Hennessy, or whatever brown liquor you like best

3 tablespoons Worcestershire sauce

2 bay leaves

1 tablespoon kosher salt, or to taste

2 large Russet potatoes, peeled and cut into 1½-inch cubes

½ pound baby carrots or sliced carrots (about 1 cup)

3 tablespoons cornstarch

1. Preheat the oven to 325°F.

2. Place the meat in a large baking dish and toss with the seasoning to coat evenly.

3. Heat the oil in a large pot or Dutch oven over medium-high heat. Add the meat in batches and sear, about 1½ minutes per side, and transfer to a large plate.

4. Add the onion to the fat in the pot and cook until tender, stirring, about 3 minutes. Add the bouillon and thyme and cook for 30 seconds,

recipe continues

stirring into the onion. Add 1½ cups of the Hennessy and stir to get all the good bits off the bottom, 30 to 45 seconds. Add 6 cups water, stir well, and return the meat to the pot.

5. Add the Worcestershire, bay leaves, and salt and stir well. Remove from the heat.

6. Cover with a tight-fitting lid or aluminum foil, transfer to the oven, and roast for 3 hours.

7. Carefully remove from the oven, uncover, and add the potatoes and carrots. Cover and continue to roast until the meat and vegetables are very tender, about 1 more hour.

8. Combine the remaining 1 cup Hennessy with the cornstarch and whisk to remove any lumps. Add the mixture to the pot and stir well to make gravy.

9. Serve hot, like I like my men.

Pot Roast Quesadilla

The way we're makin' this is the way they make quesadillas out here in LA. Read the recipe. Yes, they cook the cheese *outside* the tortilla first! And then they pile it all together and cook it again! I swear!

Double this, triple this, make as much as you want of this. You're probably gonna want more than one, I'm just sayin'.

MAKES 1 SERVING

1½ good handfuls (about 1½ cups) grated cheddar
1 large flour tortilla

½ cup leftover Sunday Pot Roast (page 132), shredded
Chopped scallions

Sour cream or Juke Joint Ranch Dressing (page 202), for serving

I. Preheat a large, heavy skillet over medium heat.

2. Sprinkle 1 handful of the cheese across the pan and cook until melted, about 30 seconds.

3. Lay the tortilla on top of the cheese and spread the pot roast and the remaining ½ handful cheese over half of the tortilla. Fold the other half of the tortilla over the meat and cheese, smash the top with a spatula, and cook for 30 seconds. Flip and cook on the other side for 30 more seconds.

4. Slide the quesadilla onto a plate, garnish with scallions (if you wanna be all LA-style), and dip in sour cream or ranch dressing.

REVERSE SEARED RIB EYE
with Juke Joint Whiskey Shrimp Scampi Sauce

Every night can be steak night at your house if you cook it this way! This reverse style of cooking is the easy way to tenderize your steaks and make 'em all sopped up and juicy. I swear once you eat steak cooked this way, you're never gonna want it cooked any other way! (And believe it or not, my daddy used to throw his steaks in the deep fryer for a completely different sopped-up flava!)

Use one large steak for a romantic meal for two. Trust me on this. Get one that's good and marbled, at least 1 inch thick, and at least a pound.

I've used a half pound of shrimp here; my favorite size is 21/25. That means there are 21 to 25 shrimp per pound, or each person gets about 6 shrimp on their steak. Tryin' to impress your man? Serve a whole pound of shrimp, hunny! Here's the thing that's most important: don't be overcookin' your shrimp or they're gonna be as tough as Joe's toenails, I tell you.

And this is my special sopped-up scampi sauce with brown liquor, baby, not that white wine everyone else be usin' for theirs. I use Hennessy in mine, 'cuz I like that cognac flava. You use whatever whiskey gets you all excited.

One 16-ounce bone-in rib eye, about 1 inch thick

1 tablespoon beef-flavored bouillon powder

1 tablespoon garlic powder

1 tablespoon onion powder

1 teaspoon kosher salt

1 teaspoon ground black pepper

2 tablespoons canola or vegetable oil

¼ cup (½ stick) salted butter

Cajun shrimp scampi sauce

¼ cup (½ stick) salted butter

2 tablespoons minced garlic or garlic paste (optional)

½ cup Hennessy or whatever brown liquor you like best

½ cup chicken broth

1 cup heavy cream

Juice of 1 lemon

½ pound shrimp, peeled and deveined

1 tablespoon Juke Joint Black Cajun Seasoning or other Cajun seasoning blend

¼ cup grated Parmesan

2 tablespoons plus 1 teaspoon minced fresh parsley

1. Preheat the oven to 275°F. Place a wire rack inside a large baking sheet.

2. Place the steak on a large plate and pat dry with paper towels on both sides to remove excess moisture, then place it on top of the rack.

3. Mix together the bouillon, garlic and onion powders, salt, and pepper in a small bowl. Sprinkle that steak real good with that, hunny. Rub it in and get it inside all the creases and crevices on both sides. Why? Because we eat both sides, OK?

4. Roast the steak (still on the rack on the baking sheet) for 30 minutes. The steak will get browned all over and tender inside.

5. Set the steak to the side for about 15 minutes while we're makin' our scampi sauce.

6. To make the sauce, heat a 12-inch cast-iron or heavy skillet over medium-high heat. Add the butter and once it's just foaming, add the garlic (if using) and cook, stirring until it's fragrant and not quite toasted, about 1 minute.

7. Add the Hennessy and stir well. Add the chicken broth and cream and cook, whisking, so that the alcohol will start to cook off a little and the sauce gets thick, 1 to 2 minutes.

8. Add the lemon juice, shrimp, and Cajun seasoning and cook, stirring, until the shrimp are just pink, about 2 minutes. Remove from the heat, stir in the Parmesan and 2 tablespoons of the parsley, and let rest while finishing the steak.

9. Meanwhile, when you add the shrimp to the pan, heat a second heavy skillet over medium-high heat until it's screaming hot.

10. Add the oil to the second pan and carefully lay down the steak. Right away—don't forget!—turn on a timer for 4 minutes or watch the clock like a hawk. And turn on that vent over the stove so the house don't blow up with smoke like it's a juke joint with everybody smokin' inside.

11. Do not move your steak until it's time to turn it. Now, I like my steak medium rare, because I am not a steak killer. I cook my steak for

recipe continues

2 minutes per side, and that means it is gonna be a perfect medium-rare temperature. Turn it once. Add the butter and use a spoon to baste the steak for about 10 seconds. Cook for another 2 minutes. (If you want your steak to be well done, then cook your steak on medium for about 7 minutes per side. If you want it medium well, then cook on medium for 4 minutes per side.)

12. Transfer the steak to a large plate for y'all to share it and top with the shrimp scampi sauce and the remaining 1 teaspoon parsley.

13. Eat it while it's hot. And wait for the love to happen once your man's got a bellyful of a good meal.

THESE SIDE DISHES

Ain't Just Some Side Chick

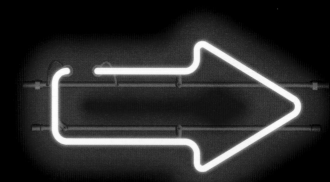

The sides of a good southern meal are like a good grandmama:

they're the glue that holds everything together.

And, hunny, I got one piece of advice: don't be showin' up to any social savings club events, baby showers, retirement parties, church socials, or whatever else you've got goin' on without our version of the Holy Trinity—potato salad, chicken salad, and pasta salad. And don't forget the paprika! You don't bring it, they gonna show you the way out!

Ole Skool
MAC 'N' CHEESE

This is a remake of my mama's recipe. The southern way, the traditional way, the way my mama made hers is with sour cream, and then she would cut blocks of cheese into it and add lotsa pepper plus paprika for color.

One reason this recipe here is so sopped up is it's layered with a rich egg custard and lots and lots of cheese. It's the cheese that has the flava, hunny! And it doesn't matter what cheese you use. Grate up what's in the fridge and mix 'em together for a pasta party! Cheddar, sharp cheddar, Gruyère, Swiss, Parmesan . . . they all like to play together!

While I make my mac in a big, deep cast-iron skillet, you can use a big casserole dish or a couple smaller ones to bake yours. Just know that your cookin' time will be different and depend on how deep you've got yours layered.

MAKES 8 SERVINGS

½ cup (1 stick) plus 1 tablespoon salted butter, cut into pieces

3 tablespoons chicken-flavored bouillon

1 pound elbow pasta

¾ cup sour cream

1 tablespoon kosher salt

1 teaspoon paprika

½ teaspoon ground black pepper

7 good handfuls (about 7 cups) grated cheddar and/or sharp cheddar, or whatever you like best

2 large eggs

2 cups whole milk

1½ cups heavy cream

2 tablespoons House Seasoning Blend (page 200) or Juke Joint Seasoning

I. Preheat the oven to 350°F. Grease a very deep 12-inch cast-iron skillet, or 9 × 13-inch casserole dish, with 1 tablespoon of the butter.

2. Combine 4 quarts (16 cups) of water and the bouillon in a large pot and bring to a boil over high heat. Add the macaroni and return to a boil,

recipe continues

stir, and cook until just al dente—that's not quite tender, y'all, but still just a little bit firm—6 to 7 minutes.

3. Drain the pasta well in a colander and transfer to a large bowl. Tuck the remaining stick of butter down real good into the pasta to get it all melted and sopped up. Add the sour cream, salt, ½ teaspoon of the paprika, and the pepper and stir it in real good. Then add in 3 handfuls (about 3 cups) of the cheese.

4. To make the custard, in a separate bowl, whisk together the eggs, milk, and cream.

5. Put about one-third of the pasta into the prepared skillet or casserole dish and top with a good handful of cheese and about 2 teaspoons of the seasoning over the top to cover.

6. Pour one-third of the custard mixture over the pasta in the skillet.

7. Repeat with the remaining ingredients, adding another two layers of pasta, then cheese and seasoning, and custard, finishing with a final handful of cheese on top. Sprinkle the top with the remaining ½ teaspoon paprika for that good color.

8. Place the skillet or casserole dish on the middle rack of the oven, with a large baking sheet on the bottom rack to catch any drips. Bake until hot and bubbly, and the custard is cooked all the way through, about 40 minutes.

9. Remove from the oven and let rest for 10 to 15 minutes before serving.

Seafood POTATO SALAD

My mama's specialty! You know potato salad ain't potato salad without hard-boiled eggs. I cook my eggs and shrimp in the same pot with the potatoes to get 'em sopped up with all that seasoning! Plus, that way, everything's ready at the same time. Make sure you set a timer when you put in the potatoes, so you don't forget about those shrimp—they're what makes this a *seafood* potato salad! The crabmeat adds a rich flavor, but if that's out of season or too rich for your pocketbook, leave it out.

Y'all know I'm not a big fan of mayonnaise, but it's what you need here. If you like that stuff, then add more. Same thing with all the rest—season this up the way you folks like it.

MAKES 8 SERVINGS

- 3 large Russet potatoes, peeled and cut into 1-inch pieces
- ¼ cup chicken-flavored bouillon powder
- 5 large eggs
- 3 tablespoons House Seasoning Blend (page 200) or Juke Joint Seasoning
- 2 tablespoons Old Bay Seasoning

- 1½ pounds shrimp, peeled and deveined
- 2 cups mayonnaise (I like Duke's)
- ½ cup sweet pickle relish
- 3 tablespoons yellow mustard
- 3 to 4 tablespoons sugar, depending on your taste (yes, you need it)

- 1 tablespoon fresh lemon juice
- 2 teaspoons kosher salt
- 1 teaspoon paprika, plus more for garnish
- 1 cup lump crabmeat, picked over to remove any shells and cartilage (optional)

I. Place the potatoes and bouillon in a large pot with enough water to cover by 2 inches. Bring to a boil over high heat. Drop the heat to a low boil, add the eggs, 2 tablespoons of the House Seasoning, and the Old Bay and cook until the potatoes are just beginning to get fork-tender, about 10 minutes.

2. Add your shrimp to the pot at this point and cook until they're just pink, about 2 minutes.

recipe continues

These Side Dishes Ain't Just Some Side Chick

Don't overcook everything! Your potatoes should be just fork-tender and not falling apart.

3. Drain in a large colander and let cool completely.

4. Peel the eggs (see No Peelin' Hard-Boiled Eggs on page 65). Dice up 4 of them, and then slice the fifth one and save it for a garnish.

5. Chop the shrimp into ½-inch pieces.

6. Combine the diced eggs, mayo, pickle relish, mustard, sugar, remaining 1 tablespoon Juke Joint Seasoning, the lemon juice, salt, and paprika in a large bowl and stir well, mashing up the yolks into the dressing. Taste and then adjust how you like it. Add the potatoes and shrimp and stir well to get it all sopped up. Adjust the seasoning again. Add the crabmeat if you're using that. Arrange the egg slices on top for decoration and sprinkle with paprika.

7. Cover and refrigerate until ready to serve. (This will keep up to 2 days in the refrigerator.)

POT LIQUOR GREENS

Who needs another greens recipe? You do. And you're gonna want this one, 'cuz instead of the collards that everyone makes, I use turnip greens, which are much sweeter and more tender. One of my favorite things in the world is cabbage, so we're addin' cabbage to these greens, too, and you get the best of both worlds.

And if you're like me, you're gonna wanna drink this pot liquor, it's so good. So go ahead and serve you up a cup.

MAKES 6 SERVINGS

12 to 16 ounces turnip greens, tough bottom stems removed

1 small to medium head green cabbage

One 2½-pound smoked turkey leg

¼ cup apple cider vinegar, or more to taste

¼ cup House Seasoning Blend (page 200) or Juke Joint Seasoning, or to taste

2 tablespoons beef-flavored bouillon powder

2 tablespoons brown sugar

1 tablespoon baking soda

Hot sauce, for serving

1. Gotta baptize your greens, hunny, and wash 'em at least three times 'cuz they so dirty and full of sand. When you think they're clean, rinse 'em one mo' time. Leave 'em whole and set aside.

2. Using a large, heavy knife, cut the cabbage in half and then in quarters. Cut away that tough white piece (the core) from each quarter. Thinly slice the cabbage into shreds.

3. Place the turkey leg in a large pot or Dutch oven with enough water to cover by 2 inches. Cover and bring to a boil. Reduce the heat to medium and cook, covered, at a low boil until fork-tender, about 2 hours.

4. Remove from the heat, uncover, and transfer the leg to a plate to rest. When cool enough to handle, pull the meat off the bone.

5. Now add your greens and cabbage to the same pot and bring to a boil.

6. Reduce the heat to a simmer and cook, covered, for 30 minutes.

7. Uncover and add the vinegar, seasoning, bouillon, brown sugar, baking soda, and the turkey leg meat. Return to a simmer and cook until the greens are soft and tender, about 15 more minutes.

8. Serve with a few dashes of hot sauce.

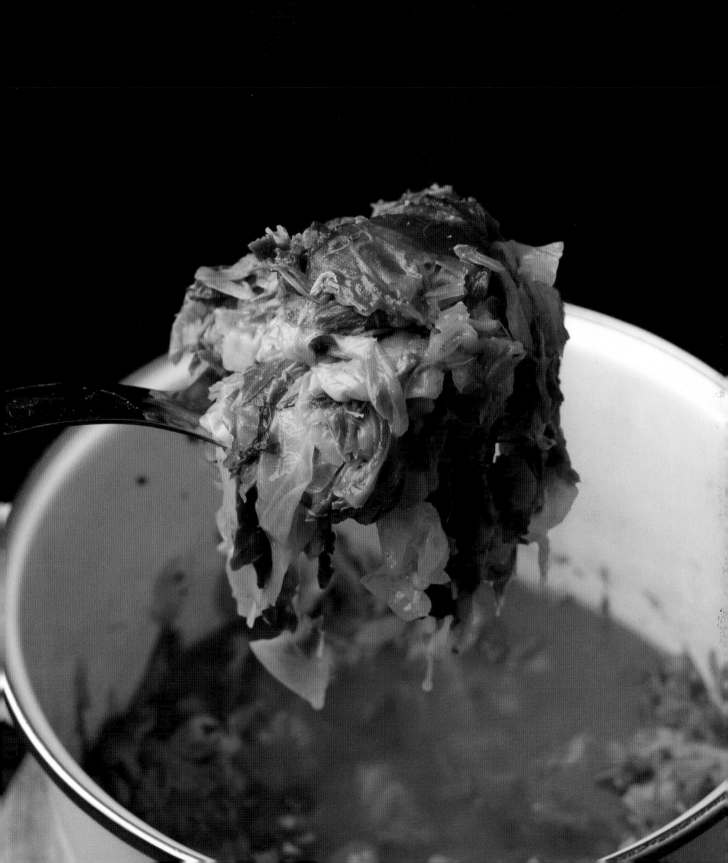

Ole Skool
SOUTHERN CANDIED YAMS

Hunny, these taste just like the ones your granmama used to make when you was little, and you been cravin' them every day since. And even though we all call these yams, the variety we find in the store are really sweet potatoes. But let's just keep callin' 'em what we call 'em. You know what I mean.

Couple words of caution: sweet potatoes (or yams) are hard and tough; be careful when you go to slice these. My mama and grandma always cut the potatoes really thin. Cut this way, they melt in ya mouth like butta! They're sweet and creamy with hints of cinnamon flava and a salty finish. I could eat a whole pot.

And do not bake them—you cannot make authentic candied yams in the oven!

MAKES 4 TO 6 SERVINGS

2 pounds sweet potatoes, peeled and thinly sliced

1 cup packed brown sugar

1 cup white sugar

1 tablespoon ground cinnamon

2 teaspoons kosher salt

2 teaspoons pure vanilla extract

½ cup (1 stick) salted butter, cut into pieces

I. Place a heavy, medium pot over medium-low heat. Add 2 tablespoons water and pile in half the sweet potato slices. Top with half each of the brown and white sugars, cinnamon, salt, and vanilla. Repeat with the remaining ingredients. Partially cover the pot, leaving about 1 inch for the steam to escape. If you cover it up, the sweet potatoes can't breathe, and they need to breathe, I promise.

2. Let the mixture come to a slow boil, about 10 minutes. Remove the lid and, with a big fork or spoon, carefully turn only the top layer of potatoes, leaving all the potatoes underneath alone. Now this bubbly sugar is hot as lava, so be careful not to mess with it too much or burn yourself.

recipe continues

These Side Dishes Ain't Just Some Side Chick

3. Don't touch the pot no matter how much you want to! Let 'em be and cook until the potatoes are nice and tender, 10 to 15 minutes.

4. Remove from the heat and let sit until the mixture stops bubbling, about 6 minutes.

5. Add the butter, cover with the lid, and let sit until the butter is melted all down and sopped up, about 5 minutes.

6. Serve good and hot, hunny.

Brown Butta
SWEET POTATO & PECAN PANCAKES

Some people like to eat breakfast all damn day—for dinner, too—this dish is for them! It's also a great brunch dish. And I have a big love for pancakes—I cannot stand waffles! The only waffles I like are the pecan waffles from Waffle House. If waffles ain't coming outta that dirty black waffle iron at Waffle House, I don't want them!

These pancakes are extra double delicious, y'all, if you've got some Ole Skool Southern Candied Yams left over from your holiday dinner. Heat those up in the microwave so they get soft, and then mash 'em up in a bowl. It's OK for them to be kinda chunky, 'cuz you wanna taste that sweet potato.

If you don't have candied yams, then make a mashed sweet potato. Cook a large sweet potato in the microwave on high (poke holes in it first so it doesn't explode!) until soft, about 10 minutes, and then scoop out the flesh and mash it.

We've got whole milk instead of water for the pancake mix and a lotta butta . . . that's what makes this extra sopped up! You'll use a stick for your brown butta, a stick for the pan to make those sopped-up edges like I like, and then a half stick for slathering all over your pancakes. And you can use more if you want!

MAKES 10 TO 12 PANCAKES

1¼ cups (2½ sticks) salted butter

2½ cups pancake mix, whichever one you like

1½ teaspoons ground cinnamon

2 cups whole milk

1 cup mashed Ole Skool Southern Candied Yams (page 151), warmed slightly until soft, or cooked, peeled, and mashed sweet potato

1 cup chopped pecans

Sopped-Up Butter Syrup (page 45) or your favorite syrup

Powdered sugar, for serving

1. Preheat the oven to warm, or about 200°F. Place a wire rack inside a large baking pan and set it next to the stovetop.

2. We're gonna make our brown butta first. Place 1 stick of the butter in a small saucepan or skillet over medium-low heat and cook until it turns the color of light brown sugar, about 3 minutes. Don't walk away from this pan! The butter can burn faster than a cheap cigarette! The butter's gonna brown real fast and get nice and foamy, and then it's gonna turn a caramel color and you're gonna smell it and it's gonna smell so doggone good, y'all. Once it's like that, pull it from the heat and let it cool some.

3. Whisk together the pancake mix and cinnamon in a large bowl. Add the milk and cooled brown butta and then whisk that up just to combine. The batter will be thick. Be careful not to overmix; leave those lumps, they'll disappear in the pan.

4. Add in the mashed candied yams and work 'em in with a rubber spatula, but not too much; you want them still all chunky so you can tell they're in there.

5. Heat a large cast-iron or heavy skillet over medium heat, about 2 minutes. Add about a tablespoon or so of the remaining butter and let it get foamy.

6. Spoon a heaping ¼ cup batter—or more if you like—into the pan. You can cook as many pancakes as will fit, depending on how big you want them and the size of your pan. I usually use a 12-inch pan and cook two at a time. Top with a couple teaspoons of the chopped pecans, or however much you like. Let it sit until bubbles start to pop on top and the edges and bottom are browned, about 2 minutes. Flip with a spatula and cook on the other side until golden brown and cooked through, 1½ to 2 minutes. Put that pancake on the rack next to the stove and place the rack in the oven to keep the pancakes warm.

7. Repeat with the rest of the batter, using more butter with each one, and then keeping them warm in the oven until you're ready to put together your plates.

8. To serve, stack up a couple pancakes on everybody's plate and top with the remaining butter and pecans.

9. Drizzle the syrup on top, then add a li'l powdered sugar and more chopped pecans. I suggest eating these in bed on a Sunday morning, right after you watch online church—at least that's what I like to do.

BBQ BAKED BEANS
with Beef

Here's my southern baked beans recipe with beef. Yes—with beef! That's how I make them, 'cuz they ain't baked beans without that meat sopped up in there! Every Black person in the South knows that! Use more or less meat, or use ground turkey or pork sausage instead. You can taste this dish as you go and adjust the seasonings to suit you, since the meat and beans are cooked already before you stick 'em in the oven.

You can double this recipe; just use two casserole dishes.

MAKES 8 SERVINGS

½ cup (1 stick) salted butter

1 pound ground beef or turkey, or ground sausage removed from the casings

2 tablespoons House Seasoning Blend (page 200) or Juke Joint Seasoning

Two 32-ounce cans baked beans, whatever brand you like best

1 small yellow onion, diced

½ bell pepper (any color), stemmed, seeded, and diced

2 cups packed brown sugar

1¼ cups Juke Joint Whiskey BBQ Sauce (page 204), or whatever you like

¾ cup yellow mustard

¼ cup Worcestershire sauce

2 tablespoons garlic powder

1 tablespoon ground black pepper, or more if you're like my daddy

1 teaspoon ground cinnamon

Couple dashes liquid smoke, to give it that BBQ essence, or mo' if you like that flava

1. Preheat the oven to 375°F. Grease a large casserole dish or cast-iron skillet with 1 tablespoon of the butter.

2. Melt 4 tablespoons of the butter in a large skillet over medium heat. Add the meat and seasoning, and cook, stirring, until well browned. Remove from the heat and let cool slightly.

3. Combine the meat and the beans, onion, bell pepper, brown sugar, BBQ sauce, mustard, Worcestershire, garlic powder, pepper, cinnamon, and liquid smoke in a large bowl. Pour into the prepared casserole dish and dot the top with the remaining 3 tablespoons butter.

4. Bake, uncovered, until bubbly and thick, about 1 hour. Let cool slightly before serving.

◆

Danni's Juke Joint Comfort Food

CHEESY BROCCOLI & RICE CASSEROLE
with Potato Chip Topping

This go-to casserole is a great way to use up leftover rice. But if you don't have any, that's OK! I've given you a Basic Rice recipe, just in case.

You wanna get fancy with this? Then add some Gouda or Gruyère, or get creative and mix it up with any kinda cheese you got in the fridge, hunny! Just don't use that bougie mozzarella. It don't taste like anything! Don't waste those calories! Can I get an amen?

MAKES 8 TO 10 SERVINGS

Basic Rice (page 210), or 3 cups leftover rice

Two 12-ounce packages frozen broccoli

Two 10.5-ounce cans cream of chicken soup

2 cups chicken broth

4 good handfuls grated cheese (about 4 cups), such as sharp cheddar, Colby Jack, or whatever you like best

2 tablespoons House Seasoning Blend (page 200) or Juke Joint Seasoning

¼ cup (½ stick) plus 1 tablespoon cold salted butter, cut into pieces

1½ cups crushed plain or sour cream and onion potato chips

1 tablespoon dried parsley (a.k.a. Black folks' glitter)

1 teaspoon garlic powder

1 teaspoon onion powder

I. Make your rice and set it aside, covered, to keep warm. (If you're using leftover rice, microwave it in a bowl, covered with plastic wrap, until warm, about 40 seconds on high.)

2. Microwave the broccoli according to the package instructions, and then cook it about 1 minute longer so it's good and mushy, like my daddy liked his. You need it to fall apart in

the casserole! Let cool about a minute before draining so you avoid a facial steam.

3. Preheat the oven to 375°F. Lightly grease a 9 × 13-inch casserole dish or large cast-iron skillet with cooking spray.

4. Combine the warm rice, broccoli, chicken soup, chicken broth, and 3 handfuls (about 3 cups) of the cheese in a large bowl and stir

recipe continues

until nice and creamy. Add the seasoning and ¼ cup of the cold butter ('cuz that's gonna melt while this is cooking and make it all sopped up and good, hunny!). Stir well.

5. Pour the mixture in the prepared pan and then top with the remaining 1 handful cheese. Bake until hot all the way through and the cheese is bubbly on top, 25 to 30 minutes. Remove from the oven and let rest for 10 minutes.

6. To make the topping, melt the remaining 1 tablespoon butter in a small skillet over medium heat. Reduce the heat to medium-low, add the potato chip crumbs, parsley, and garlic and onion powders. Cook, stirring, until the mixture is lightly toasted and fragrant, 3 to 5 minutes.

7. Sprinkle the potato chip mixture evenly over the hot casserole and dig in!

Sour Cream & Onion
MASHED POTATOES

When I was growing up, my mama would always cook instant potatoes and add butter, sour cream, and cheese to them—they were always so good! She would pair those potatoes with a fried pork chop or fried chicken for a weeknight dinner, and we would be as happy as a woman in a Chanel store with an unlimited budget. Yup, that good!

This time we ain't using instant; we are gettin' a little fancier with red potatoes. Since these have sweet skins, we ain't peelin' 'em. But potatoes are really dirty, so make sure you wash 'em well and get 'em clean. We're also gettin' fancy by adding Parmesan for richness. You can add any melting cheese here—Fontina, Gouda, and white cheddar are good choices.

I serve these with my Sunday Pot Roast with Cognac Gravy (page 132) or Spatchcocked Whole Fried Chicken (page 113). Men also *love* these potatoes with the Reverse Seared Rib Eye with Juke Joint Whiskey Shrimp Scampi Sauce (page 136).

MAKES 6 SERVINGS

3 pounds small to medium red potatoes, halved

One 1-ounce envelope onion soup mix

1 cup half-and-half, or more as needed

¾ cup sour cream, or more as needed

1½ to 2 good handfuls (1½ to 2 cups) grated Parmesan or whatever you like best

2 tablespoons dried parsley

1 tablespoon onion powder

¼ cup (½ stick) salted butter, cut into pieces, at room temperature

Kosher salt and ground black pepper to taste

These Side Dishes Ain't Just Some Side Chick

1. Place the potatoes and soup mix in a large pot with enough water to cover by 1 inch and bring to a boil. Reduce the heat and simmer until fork-tender but not breaking apart, 12 to 15 minutes.

2. Remove from the heat and drain in a colander. Don't worry: the onion from the soup mix will stay with the potatoes.

3. Return the potatoes to the pot and place over low heat to dry the potatoes a little, 15 to 20 seconds.

4. While still over low heat, mash the potatoes with a heavy fork or potato masher until just creamy but still a little chunky. I love a good cellulite potato, no shame in my game. If you prefer a smoother potato, then keep on mashing or even use a food mill. I ain't judgin'.

5. Stir the half-and-half into the potatoes and mix well. Add in the sour cream, Parmesan, parsley, and onion powder and mix well. It should now be nice and creamy.

6. Add in the butta and stir until it gets really sopped up in those potatoes. Taste and adjust the seasonings as needed with salt and pepper. If you want creamier potatoes, add more half-and-half; if you prefer more tang, add in a little more sour cream.

7. Serve these hot!

Easy as Hell
LAZY GARLIC BREAD

I love this bread so much! It only takes a couple minutes to make, and it's perfect every time. I got this recipe from my mama, too! And no, your country behind can't use sandwich bread for this. You need a loaf of French or Italian bread, so it gets all crispy and crunchy around the edges as it bakes and is still soft and chewy in the middle.

MAKES 2 TO 6 SERVINGS, DEPENDING ON IF YOU WANNA SHARE!

1 loaf French or Italian bread, sliced in half lengthwise

½ cup (1 stick) salted butter, at room temperature

2 tablespoons garlic powder

2 tablespoons dried parsley

1 tablespoon onion powder

1½ teaspoons ground black pepper

1½ teaspoons paprika

1. Preheat the oven to 325°F.

2. Lay the bread halves, cut side up, on a baking sheet and spread with the softened butter.

3. Mix the garlic powder, parsley, onion powder, pepper, and paprika in a small bowl. If you want your bread to have more color, then add more paprika. If you want it to have a bold onion flava, then add more onion powder, and so on! This bread is super easy and there ain't no right or wrong way to do it—just don't burn it!

4. Sprinkle the seasoning over the bread and bake until golden brown with crispy edges, 7 to 10 minutes. Cut it up how you like it and serve this any time of the week with anything! It's a Stevie Wonder hit!

These Side Dishes Ain't Just Some Side Chick

Just a Li'l
SOMETHIN'
SWEET

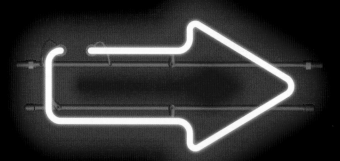

You can be full as a tick, but where I'm from, we always got room for a li'l somethin' sweet!

The classic line before dessert is, "I know I ain't got no business eatin' this . . ." But of course, we do it anyway.

Y'all probably thinking: "Oh Lord, Danni over there on Food Network judgin' them big old cakes, and we wanna know if they sopped up. Well, hunny, I am a girl who will never kiss and tell. But I will say, you ain't gotta ever worry about us baking those type of cakes over here, because down in the South we like to keep everything low-key, including our cakes. So you're gonna get simple, delicious desserts and some old tips that I've learned over the years from my mama and aunties. Let's get baking, y'all.

BROWNIE SWIRL POUND CAKE
with Cream Cheese Icing

Everybody loves church lady pound cake—I mean, what's not to love about a rich, buttery, moist slice of decadent goodness? But I must also tell you, I love a good ole brownie, too. One tipsy Saturday morning after too many mimosas, my girls and I needed something sweet. So, some type of way, a box of brownie mix and a homemade cake batter ended up meeting each other, and they made this delicious baby here. Don't worry, I've cut down the sugar a bit to make sure it ain't too sweet. There is nothing worse than a dessert that makes you feel like you are about to enter a diabetic coma.

And I tell you what—this is the best cake recipe made with that cake flour; it's so tender, plus you don't have to go through the extra work of sifting (see Baking Tips, page 171). This cake is so moist and decadent, y'all, it's downright sinful!

MAKES 1 BUNDT CAKE, 12 TO 16 SERVINGS

1 box (about 18 ounces) fudgy-style brownie mix

2 tablespoons canola or vegetable oil (optional)

1 cup (2 sticks) salted butter, at room temperature

1 cup sugar

5 tablespoons butter-flavored shortening

6 large eggs, at room temperature

3 cups cake flour

Cream cheese icing

½ cup (4 ounces) cream cheese, at room temperature

2 cups powdered sugar

⅓ cup heavy cream or milk, at room temperature

¼ teaspoon pure vanilla extract

I. Preheat the oven to 325°F. Now this next step is extra important, 'cuz you won't wanna try to turn your cake outta the pan later and find it won't come out. Grease your Bundt cake pan really well. I like to use that baking spray with flour (such as Baker's Joy). If you wanna go ole skool, then grease yours with about 1 tablespoon extra butter and then shake around 1 tablespoon flour to coat the sides,

recipe continues

knocking out the excess into the sink when you're done.

2. Make the brownie batter according to the package instructions. Just whisk it all up in a big bowl like they tell you to do. And add that extra 2 tablespoons of oil if you want and see if my tip (see Baking Tips, page 171) is right about a moister cake.

3. Combine the butter, sugar, and shortening in a large bowl. (The shortening is the secret ingredient. Make sure you get the butter-flavored kind; that's the one that adds all that sopped-up flavor everybody loves!) Using a hand mixer on medium speed, beat the ingredients together until creamy, about 3 minutes. Add the eggs one at a time, alternating with the flour, beating on medium after each addition just to combine. Scrape down the sides as needed and beat on medium until smooth, 10 to 15 seconds.

4. Spoon about one-third of the pound cake batter into the prepared pan so that the bottom of the pan is just covered. Top with half the brownie batter, spooning it a little around the top of the pound cake batter. Cover that with half the remaining pound cake mixture and then the remaining brownie batter. Last, you're gonna add the rest of the pound cake batter to the top, spooning it around so that it covers the brownie mix and the top is smooth. Tap the cake pan on the countertop a couple times to get rid of any air bubbles.

5. Bake until golden brown on the top and set and a toothpick inserted into the center of the pound cake comes out clean, about 1 hour 20 minutes. (The brownie batter will still be slightly wet, but it will firm up as the cake cools.)

6. Remove the cake from the oven and let cool for 10 minutes in the pan. This is important, y'all—let that cake be!

7. To remove from the pan, place a large plate upside down over the top of the cake and with one hand holding the bottom of the cake pan (use a potholder or kitchen towel), flip it so the bottom of the cake pan is now on top. Let sit for the cake to release onto the plate.

8. Cool the cake completely at room temperature, about 30 minutes, before icing. (If you're not icing it, you still need to let it cool before slicing it. Trust me on this, don't be hardheaded.)

9. Meanwhile, make your icing. Place the cream cheese in a large bowl and beat with a hand mixer on medium speed until creamy. Turn off the mixer and add the powdered sugar. Beat on low to combine. Add the cream and vanilla and beat on medium until smooth. That's it, y'all!

10. With a spoon, drizzle the glaze over the top of the cooled cake and then serve it up!

BAKING TIPS

My mama taught me to use cake flour when baking. Why cake flour? Cake flour has a lower protein content and makes a more tender cake.

She never sifts hers, so I don't sift mine and it comes out fine every time. If you wanna take the extra step to sift, then do it.

You can use all-purpose flour here, if that's what you got. Just know the texture will be a bit denser. If you use all-purpose, sift it before you measure it, and then remeasure and sift it again before you add it to the batter.

This extra step will aerate—see what I did there, I just used a big word—and lighten up the all-purpose flour.

And here's a little thing that I do when I make my brownie mix: I always add 2 tablespoons of extra oil to the batter, even if not called for in the box instructions. I just feel like it gives the batter a little moisture insurance lol. Try it and see!

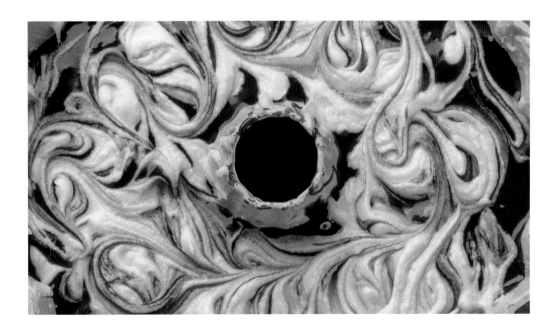

Sweet
PO-PUMPKIN PIE

This creation was inspired by some of my friends who like pumpkin pie. And yes, y'all, they are Black! They aren't southern either, even though that still don't give them a pass. I prefer sweet potato for my pie. But oddly enough, I learned from my mama that my granmama Kat would use a little canned pumpkin in her sweet potato pie to stretch it. Hell, when you got eight kids, you gotta do what you gotta do.

And honestly, after making this—I hate to admit this as a southern Black cook—I swear the texture of this pie is dynamite! It's creamy and buttery, and you can't taste the pumpkin at all. Please don't take my Black card for this . . . Just try it first and then let's talk!

You can use a store-bought crust, but get a good brand—the crust matters. I like the Marie Callender's "made from scratch" *frozen* pie crusts. There's no need to thaw them, but you do want to parbake them! This is a trick I learned from my mama and my auntie Joann. They both make really good sweet potato pies, and they told me growing up that you always wanna bake your crust a little bit before you add your filling. This will keep the crusts from being undercooked and gummy; instead they'll be soft and tender. Use refrigerated crusts if you'd prefer—just cut the cooking time by a minute or so.

And if you don't wanna make two pies, you can freeze the leftover filling for another time. Thaw it in the fridge and whisk well before using. The filling will keep frozen for up to 3 months.

PS—You can also cut this pie into small chunks and add it to my No Churn, No Fuss Ice Cream (page 190), which will taste like sweet potato pie ice cream. Chile, it's incredible! Thank me later.

2 frozen or refrigerated deep-dish pie crusts, packaging removed

2 large sweet potatoes, about 1 pound each

1 cup (2 sticks) salted butter

1 cup packed brown sugar

¾ cup white sugar

2 large eggs

2 tablespoons ground cinnamon

2 teaspoons ground nutmeg

1½ teaspoons kosher salt

1 teaspoon pure vanilla extract

One 15-ounce can pure pumpkin

1 cup heavy cream

2 tablespoons all-purpose flour

I. Preheat the oven to 350°F.

2. Bake the pie crusts on the middle rack of the oven until they're the color of sand, 7 to 8 minutes. Place on a wire rack to cool completely.

3. Increase the oven temperature to 425°F.

4. Place the potatoes on a baking sheet or in a casserole dish and roast until fork-tender, 45 minutes to 1 hour. The skin should be a little wrinkly, and don't worry if it has some burn marks on it—that's the sugar caramelizing, hunny. (Or cook the sweet potatoes in the microwave on high—poke holes in 'em first so they don't explode—until soft, 10 to 12 minutes.)

5. Transfer the sweet potatoes to a plate and let sit until cool enough to handle, 10 to 20 minutes, then peel the potatoes.

6. Reduce the oven temperature to 350°F.

7. Meanwhile, brown the butta. Place the butter in a medium saucepan over medium-low and cook until it's the color of light brown sugar, 3 to 5 minutes. Don't walk away from this pan! The butter's gonna brown real fast and get nice and foamy and then turn a nice caramel color

and smell so doggone good. Remove from the heat and let cool some.

8. To make the pie (finally!), place the peeled, roasted sweet potatoes in a large bowl and mix with a hand mixer on medium speed until smooth, 45 seconds to 1 minute. (You can also do this in a stand mixer, if you got one.)

9. Add in your cooled brown butta and mix on medium speed until the sweet potatoes are saturated and gettin' all sopped up with that good brown butta flava, about 45 seconds.

10. Add the brown and white sugars and mix on medium speed to whip up the sweet potato mixture as much as possible, about 2 minutes. (This is important: it can help prevent strings in your pie, and, hunny, trust me, potato pie with strings ain't nuthin' nice.)

II. Add in your eggs, cinnamon, nutmeg, salt, and vanilla and mix until well combined, 1 minute, scraping down the sides of the bowl as needed, 'cuz we don't want any ingredients hanging around like they at a cookout.

12. Add the pumpkin, cream, and flour and mix well, 1 minute.

recipe continues

13. You can taste it at this point and add whatever you think it needs more of. Yes, I know there is raw egg in it, but no one is telling you to eat the whole doggone bowl. A pinch won't hurt you—live on the wild side a little.

14. Once the pie filling tastes great TO YOU, divide the batter between the pie shells, filling them barely to the top, right below the decorative pie edges. This can sometimes be tricky, so I like to use a 1-cup measuring cup to help. I pour 1 cup into the first pie shell, then 1 cup into the second shell, and I go back 'n' forth until the filling is gone. Doing it this way helps divide the filling evenly . . . at least that's my theory. Just make sure you don't go above the decorative pie edges because the pies will rise slightly while they bake, and, chile, you are asking for a whole lot of oven cleanup.

15. Now, if you are only making 1 pie, then just fill the 1 pie shell and freeze the remaining batter in a plastic bowl with a lid or a freezer bag.

16. Bake the pies on the middle rack until a toothpick comes out clean, 45 to 50 minutes. (If you don't have a toothpick, use the tip of a knife; that's what my mama does.)

17. Let cool on a wire rack for at least 1 hour before slicing. Cutting into a hot pie is like jumping in a pool without waterproof mascara; you about to be looking like a damn raccoon, stuff just running everywhere—same with this pie. Let it be.

18. Slice it up and serve warm. I like to eat my pie cold, so I refrigerate it overnight. I top it with a little whipped cream or Cool Whip and powdered sugar, and enjoy it with a cup of hot coffee. That's absolutely divine! When I take a bite, it makes me feel like I am sitting at a Black-owned bougie coffee and pastry café. And I'm here for it!

Church Lady
CANDIED APPLES

This recipe is really dear to my heart. Not only 'cuz it's good, but it takes me back down memory lane. One thing I learned growing up in Birmingham, Alabama, is that everybody loves good candied apples! And the people who made the best candied apples back then were the Black Baptist church ladies on the nurses' guild. Y'all know what I'm talkin' about—the guild ladies wore all white on Sundays and sat in the back row of the church. If somebody shout and pass out, here comes a lady from the nurses to put something under that person's nose, and then they'd shout and come back to life, even though it was the Holy Ghost that made them do it. The funny thing is they called themselves nurses, but no one had a degree. Black people just be doing anything and calling it something, chile.

Two things about candied apples. First, they're healthy 'cuz they're fruit! Second, if you do 'em right, the sweetness will balance with the tartness of the apple and it'll do your inner soul some good! They're so addictive and delicious!

These are easy to make. And you can get your kids to help—just keep them away from the candying, hot syrup part. You don't wanna have people talk about you later on, 'cuz you know they will.

MAKES 6 SERVINGS

6 medium apples (I like Honeycrisp, but use any sweet apples you like)

2 cups sugar

½ cup corn syrup

2 teaspoons red food coloring (choose the kind that comes in the 1-ounce bottle, not the tiny pointy-hat bottles)

> **Note** You'll need 6 Popsicle sticks or other wooden sticks and a candy thermometer.

1. Remove the stems from the apples and wash and dry well. Insert a Popsicle stick into the center of each one, pushing about halfway down into the apple. No need to core these or do anything else! If you can't find Popsicle sticks or haven't been savin' yours, use those heavy kebab sticks; just be careful with the sharp points.

2. Cover a large baking sheet with wax paper.

3. Combine ¾ cup water, the sugar, corn syrup, and food coloring in a large, heavy pot. Do not stir! Stick a candy thermometer in there and clip it to the side of the pot. Bring to a boil over medium-high heat and cook without stirring until the mixture reaches the hard crack stage, 300° to 310°F. This should take 15 to 20 minutes and you have to be patient.

4. Carefully remove from the heat and let sit until the syrup stops bubbling, about 20 seconds.

5. One at a time, hold each apple by its Popsicle stick and dip into the hot syrup—and be careful, y'all, this stuff will burn somethin' awful—turnin' to coat real good, so it's dressed up all over. Place the coated apples on the wax paper and let cool completely, at least 20 minutes.

6. When the apples are cool and the sugar has hardened, you can wrap these in plastic wrap like the church ladies do and store them in the fridge for up to 1 week if you don't want to eat them right away!

RED VELVET SHEET CAKE
with Cream Cheese Icing

Red velvet is my favorite cake in the world. Period. So you know this recipe is going to be the best one you've ever made because it's personal. I'm gonna tell you now, this is delicious.

When I was growing up, Miss Washington would always make sheet cakes for every church occasion. And it's easy—shit, you can't mess up a sheet cake. Plus, you can serve up a whole lotta people without a whole lotta work.

Buy the McCormick's food coloring that comes in the bigger 1-ounce bottle, or your supermarket's brand that's in the bigger bottle. Those little pointy-hat bottles don't turn the cake the right color we're goin' for here. And use aluminum foil to line your pan, 'cuz you gonna be icing and serving the cake straight from that pan. That way, the knife you use to cut the cake ain't gonna be scrapin' up your pan and ruinin' it for next time.

If by some wild chance you got some leftover cake, cut this into individual servings, wrap it in plastic, and freeze with the icing on top. To serve, unwrap and thaw at room temperature.

Last direction up here: a red velvet cake needs to be decorated with pecans. But, hunny, if you allergic to pecans, I ain't got a check to write you; don't be adding 'em to yours now.

2½ cups cake flour (See Baking Tips, page 171)

2 cups sugar

1 tablespoon cocoa powder

1 teaspoon baking soda

1 teaspoon kosher salt

1½ cups whole buttermilk, at room temperature (I always use a lot of buttermilk to make the cake extra moist and tender)

1¼ cups canola or vegetable oil

2 large eggs, at room temperature

1 teaspoon pure vanilla extract

1 teaspoon distilled white vinegar

1 tablespoon plus 1 teaspoon red food coloring, such as McCormick's

Cream Cheese Icing (recipe follows)

1 cup chopped pecans, or more if you like

1. Preheat the oven to 350°F. Line a 14 × 10 × 1-inch jelly roll pan with aluminum foil and spray with baking spray.

2. Combine the flour, sugar, cocoa, baking soda, and salt in a large bowl and whisk to combine.

3. Combine the buttermilk, oil, eggs, vanilla, vinegar, and food coloring in another large bowl and whisk to combine. Add the dry ingredients to the wet and whisk until just combined, 30 seconds.

4. Pour the batter into the prepared pan and bake until tender and a toothpick inserted in the center comes out clean, about 25 minutes.

5. Ole skool trick: sweat the cake before you ice it; that'll keep it moist. When the cake comes outta the oven, let it cool undisturbed for 5 to 10 minutes, and then cover the top of the pan with plastic wrap. Let it cool completely while you make the icing. This is like liquid gold, this tip, and I'll charge you for it later. If you share this tip, then we ain't gonna be friends no mo'.

6. Unwrap the plastic from your cake and discard.

7. With a butter knife, spread the icing over the top of the cooled cake. Decorate with chopped pecans and see who comes back first for seconds and thirds!

Cream Cheese Icing

We ain't usin' no whisk for this. Get you a hand mixer, unless you lookin' to make this your exercise for the day and work off those calories you 'bout to eat, hunny.

MAKES 3 CUPS

One 8-ounce block cream cheese, at room temperature

½ cup (1 stick) salted butter, at room temperature

1 teaspoon pure vanilla extract
3½ cups powdered sugar

I. Combine the cream cheese, butter, and vanilla in a large bowl and beat with a hand mixer on medium speed until smooth, about 1 minute.

2. With the mixer off, add the powdered sugar 1 cup at a time, then blend well after each addition. After the last addition, blend on medium until the icing is smooth and thick.

3. Keep the icing at room temperature so it's easy to spread on the cake. Don't refrigerate this first.

LUNCH LADY COOKIES
a.k.a. Chocolate Chip Peanut Butter Cookies

You gonna love these biracial cookies (that's what I call it when I mix brown and white sugar together). They're just as gooey and wonderful as those fatties the lunch ladies made at my school.

Here's somethin' you may not know: I like to use bread flour because that makes a thicker, chewier cookie. You can use all-purpose for a more standard cookie—whatever you've got in the pantry. My secret ingredient to make them soft and chewy on the inside is cornstarch. Don't be tellin' anybody that!

I prefer semisweet chips to make these, but my daughter likes milk chocolate chips—go figure! Make yours with whatever you like best.

MAKES 10 BIG, FAT COOKIES

1 cup (2 sticks) salted butter

2 cups bread flour or all-purpose flour

2 tablespoons cornstarch

1 teaspoon baking soda

1 teaspoon kosher salt, plus more for sprinkling

¾ cup packed brown sugar

½ cup white sugar

2 large eggs, at room temperature

1 tablespoon pure vanilla extract

½ cup peanut butter

1½ cups semisweet or milk chocolate chips

I. Place the butter in a medium saucepan over medium heat and cook just until it's the color of light brown sugar, 3 to 5 minutes. Don't take your eyes off that butta! It'll turn into a lava mess before you can say "Merry Christmas." Remove the pan from the heat and let cool slightly until the bubbles settle down, about 5 minutes.

2. Whisk together the flour, cornstarch, baking soda, and salt in a medium bowl.

recipe continues

3. Whisk together the slightly cooled butter, brown and white sugars, eggs, and vanilla in a large bowl until well combined.

4. Using a wooden spoon or rubber spatula, fold the dry ingredients into the butter mixture and then fold in the peanut butter and then the chocolate chips. Cover and refrigerate for 30 minutes.

5. Preheat the oven to 350°F.

6. If you wanna be bougie, line a large baking sheet with parchment paper. Or if you a regular girl like me, just put those cookies directly on that sheet; they'll be fine, hunny, just watch 'em.

7. Using a ¼-cup ice cream scoop, scoop the dough onto the baking sheet.

8. Bake until light golden brown but still soft, 9 to 10 minutes.

9. Let the cookies firm up on the baking sheet for about 5 minutes. Lightly sprinkle the tops with additional salt while they're still warm.

10. Transfer with a spatula to a wire rack or large plate to cool completely.

11. Serve warm or let cool to room temperature and store in an airtight container for up to 4 days.

LUNCH LADY COOKIE ICE CREAM SANDWICHES

Now, you want somethin' even better?

Take ⅓ cup (hell—take ½ cup or ⅔ cup!) of my homemade No Churn, No Fuss Ice Cream (page 190) and smush it up between two of these cookies.

Make a whole mess of 'em until you ain't got none left.

Put everything on a plate lined with wax paper and stick in the freezer for at least 10 minutes to firm up.

Or wrap 'em in wax paper and freeze to eat later.

No Churn
BANANA PUDDING ICE CREAM

When I was growing up, the ice cream truck would come through our neighborhood on Fridays during the summertime. We always saved our dollar during the week to give to the ice cream man. And then we would eat it either on the porch or while walking down the street to Wiggins Park, the recreational center. Later, in high school, we would sit on the back of the guys' old-school Chevys and eat our ice cream. So, I've always had a love for ice cream.

Now, in the southern region, Blue Bell brand ice cream is like the crème de la crème. When you saw Blue Bell in somebody's house, you knew that it was a special treat. One of their bestsellers, outside of their cookies and cream, was banana pudding ice cream. It is so doggone good. It has chunks of vanilla wafers in it, an amazing banana flavor that isn't overpowering, and vanilla ice cream swirled throughout. Since I can't get it at home in LA, I decided to make my own version of it. And don't tell Blue Bell, but mine is actually better. And it's easy to make.

MAKES ABOUT 1 QUART

2 cups heavy cream

One 14-ounce can sweetened condensed milk

½ of a 3.4-ounce package vanilla pudding mix

2 cups crushed Nilla wafers, or more if you like your 'nana pudding extra cookie-ish, plus more for serving

½ banana, cut into small pieces (you can freeze the other half and add it to your smoothies to make them creamy and sweeter)

Sweetened whipped cream or Cool Whip, for serving (optional)

Danni's Juke Joint Comfort Food

1. Whisk together the heavy cream, condensed milk, and pudding mix in a large bowl until combined, about 1 minute or so. This doesn't take long, so you will be fine without a hand mixer, but it's exercise for ya!

2. Add the wafers and chopped banana and fold them in with a rubber spatula.

3. Pour the ice cream into a freezer-safe container (such as a metal loaf pan or heavy plastic bowl) and cover with a lid (or tightly with a layer of plastic wrap and then a layer of aluminum foil). Freeze until set, at least 4 hours or overnight.

4. Serve the next day with whipped cream if you like and more crumbled wafers. Or if you ain't got time for all that, hunny, eat it right out the bowl! Who judging you? It sholl ain't me.

NO CHURN, NO FUSS ICE CREAM
Make Your Own Flava

I love this recipe because it's such an easy way to turn a leftover dessert or a sweet snack into something completely new. All you need are two ingredients plus some leftover goodies mixed in. You can add whatever you've got or want: crumble up your favorite cookies (but keep them chunky!), cut up a big hunk of cake, or add in some of my favorite goodies like Sweet Po-Pumpkin Pie (page 172) all scooped up into pieces. Shoot! You can add any of the desserts in this book. No need to measure—just plop it in and sop it up!

MAKES 1 QUART

3 cups heavy cream, cold
One 14-ounce can sweetened
  condensed milk (see Tip)

2 nice-size slices or big chunks
  of somethin' sweet, like pie,
  cobbler, or cake, or 4 to
  5 medium cookies

I.   Put the heavy cream and sweetened condensed milk in a large bowl and make sure all that condensed milk comes out! Don't waste a drop! Whisk by hand until nicely combined, about a minute or so.

2.   Now, take your filling and chop or crumble it into bite-size pieces. Gently fold your filling into the cream mixture so it's all mixed up in there, but don't overdo it. You want the ice cream base to look like it went and got a Mommy makeover, OK? That means it should have some body to it.

3.   Pour the mixture into a freezer-safe container (like a metal loaf pan or heavy plastic bowl) and cover it with a lid (or tightly with a layer of plastic wrap and then a layer of aluminum foil). Freeze until set, at least 4 hours or overnight.

Danni's Juke Joint Comfort Food

4. Remove from the freezer and let sit at room temperature to soften slightly, about 10 minutes, so you can scoop it up.

5. Now, do what Beyoncé does, hunny, which is SERVE! Period.

> **Tip** We ain't making mac 'n' cheese, hunny. You're gonna need sweetened condensed milk, which is thick and sweet like a girl in the South, not evaporated milk (unsweetened like regular milk, only with a little more fat). And you can use heavy cream, light cream, or heavy whipping cream for this, whatever is at your store. They're all basically the same, just with a li'l bit different milk fat content.

EASY ULTIMATE LEMON ICEBOX PIE
with No Meringue

I have some opinions on meringue that I would rather not share, because I know y'all like to tussle about it. Now, tart, tangy, lemon icebox pie—that's different. This one has got a gooey butta cookie crust, icy-cool lemon filling, and a luscious whipped cream topping.

I use Nilla wafers for my crust, but you can use any cookie you want. And I use a 9-inch springform pan to make this at my house—it's deep enough to handle everything, plus the pie comes out easy. Use any 9-inch pan you got, so long as it's at least 2 inches high. If you use a 10-inch pan, just know your crust won't be as thick or the pie as high.

Only real lemons work in this recipe, not concentrate. You want your mouth to pop and your neck to snap . . . That's what I'm talkin' about, hunny!

MAKES ONE 9-INCH PIE

One 11-ounce box Nilla wafers
6 tablespoons salted butter, melted

16 ounces (that's 2 blocks, y'all) cream cheese, at room temperature
Two 14-ounce cans sweetened condensed milk

2 cups heavy cream
Juice of 5 lemons (about ½ cup; see Tip)
Sweetened whipped cream or Cool Whip, for serving

1. Preheat the oven to 350°F.

2. Place the cookies in a food processor and pulse to fine crumbs. (Or you can place the cookies in a large freezer bag, seal it tight, and crush 'em up using the back of a heavy skillet. A few chunks are alright, hunny.)

3. To make the crust, measure 1¾ cups of cookie crumbs and place them in a large bowl. (Keep the rest of the crumbs for decorating your pie or using in another recipe later.) Add the melted butter and stir it all up to moisturize those crumbs. The butter is the glue to hold the crust together.

4. Using your fingers or the bottom of a juice glass, press the crumb mixture into the bottom and slightly up the sides of a 9-inch springform pan.

5. Bake until the crust is set and golden brown, 8 to 10 minutes. Let cool to room temperature. Place in the freezer to get completely cold while you make the filling.

6. To make the filling, place the cream cheese in a large bowl and beat with a hand mixer on medium speed until smooth, about 1 minute. (It's gotta be soft; otherwise you're gonna get cellulite-lookin' lumps and dimples in your filling.) With the mixer off, add the condensed milk. It takes a minute for it all to come outta the cans, but take your time and get it out. You paid for it, plus you want all that flava in your pie! Mix that up real good on medium speed, scraping down the edges of the bowl to get it all mixed together.

7. Add your cream, turn up the mixer to high speed, and beat until smooth, about 1 minute. Turn off the mixer and add the lemon juice, then mix on low speed until well combined and really smooth, 1 to 2 minutes.

8. Remove the pie crust from the freezer and pour in the filling, scraping the bowl with a rubber spatula to make sure you get every bit. Give the pan a shake to get rid of the air bubbles.

9. Chill in the refrigerator for at least 6 hours. I like to put it in there overnight so it's good and firm. If you wanna serve your pie sooner, stick it in the freezer for at least 4 hours and then serve.

10. Slice the pie cold and serve each piece with whipped cream and crushed-up cookies on top.

> **Tip** The secret to getting the most juice outta your fresh lemons is to put 'em in the microwave for 20 seconds on high so they'll get nice and soft. Really, it releases the juices.
> Roll them on the countertop a coupla times after that, and then slice them in half and juice them into a large bowl.
>
> **And here's another tip** If you forgot to leave out your cream cheese to get soft (or don't wanna wait), unwrap both blocks, put 'em on a plate, and microwave for 30 seconds.

DRUNKEN DEEP-FRIED APPLE DUMPLINGS
à la Mode with Caramel Glaze

This recipe is so sopped up, and not because it's deep fried and smothered in a glaze. It's my favorite because its super healthy! I mean, chile, it's an apple . . . How bad can it really be? We are clearly just redefining what a whole-food diet is over here. If it just so happens to slip into a hot grease Jacuzzi, so be it—it's still filled with lots of fiber and vitamins, duh!

I often get asked to be a guest on different shows—one of my best times was makin' these dumplings on OWN! (Hunny, you've got to watch that video!) My sister says this is her favorite thing that I've ever made for her.

To cook the apples, we're making a wine poaching liquid to get 'em all drunk and delicious, chile. I use Moscato, 'cuz it's sweet like me. You can use white Zinfandel or any wine you like best. There's sugar in here, too, to sweeten it up real good. And using store-bought refrigerated (or frozen) pie crusts makes wrapping up your apples into dumplings so, so easy. Just keep the crusts in the refrigerator while you're cooking the apples and caramel; they're easier to work with when they're good and cold. If you buy frozen crusts, thaw them in the fridge till you need 'em.

MAKES 2 SERVINGS, MAYBE 4 IF YOU FEEL LIKE SHARIN'

One package of 2 premade pie crusts (about 14 ounces), either frozen or refrigerated

3 cups Moscato or white Zinfandel, or whatever you like best

1½ cups white sugar

2 tablespoons pure vanilla extract

1 tablespoon ground cinnamon

2 large, sweet apples, like Honeycrisp or Pink Lady, peeled and cored

½ cup (1 stick) salted butter

1 cup packed brown sugar

1 cup heavy cream

½ teaspoon kosher salt

Canola or vegetable oil, for frying

2 scoops No Churn, No Fuss Ice Cream (page 190), to make it even more sopped up!

Chopped pecans, for serving

1. First off, keep your pie crusts in the fridge till you're ready to use them. (If frozen, thaw them there.)

2. To make the poaching liquid, combine 4 cups water, the wine, white sugar, 1 tablespoon of the vanilla, and the cinnamon in a medium, heavy pot and bring to a low boil over medium-high heat, stirring to dissolve the sugar.

3. Carefully add the apples and return to a simmer. Cook, uncovered, turning occasionally, until the apples are good 'n' tender, about 20 minutes. And don't overcook these, 'cuz then they'll be all mushy.

4. Take the apples out with a big spoon and let 'em cool on a plate.

5. And keep that poaching liquid once it cools! You can refrigerate that in a jar and use it again for makin' cocktails or poaching more apples, peaches, or pears. This stuff is too good to waste.

6. Now we're gonna make our sopped-up caramel! In a clean medium saucepan, melt the butter over medium-high heat. Whisk in the brown sugar, reduce the heat to medium low,

and cook until dissolved. Now this is like hot food lava, baby! Be careful while it's cookin' so that it don't burn you and it doesn't burn. This'll burn fast. You just want to let it get good 'n' bubbly and melted, about 2 minutes.

7. Remove from the heat and carefully stir in the cream, whisking to combine. Again, you don't wanna get spattered with hot lava caramel, hunny; it ain't gonna be cute on your hand. Be careful while you doin' this. Add the remaining 1 tablespoon vanilla and the salt and whisk well. Put the pot back over the heat, bring to a boil, and cook for 1 minute. It's that easy.

8. Remove from the heat and let cool while you're puttin' the dumplings together.

9. Unwrap 1 pie crust on a large cutting board or clean counter and roll into an 11-inch circle. (I usually don't flour my counter when I do this, but if your pie dough seems like it will stick, just add about 2 tablespoons of flour to your counter and then lay the dough on top.) Place 1 cooked apple in the center and wrap it with the crust on

all sides, like a present. Stick two toothpicks into the excess crust at the top to secure the crust around the apple. Repeat with the second pie crust and apple, securing with toothpicks.

10. Place a wire rack inside a large baking sheet and place it next to the stovetop.

11. Meanwhile, add enough oil to come halfway up the sides of a large, heavy pot or deep-fat fryer and heat to 350°F over medium-high heat. When the oil is shimmering, carefully lower 1 wrapped apple into the oil using a long-handled spoon or fryer basket and cook until the crust is deep golden brown and cooked through and the apple floats to the top, 3 to 4 minutes. Transfer to the prepared wire rack to drain. Repeat with the second apple, letting the oil return to 350°F before putting it in the oil.

12. Place the apples on two serving plates and drizzle with the caramel sauce. Sop it up with a scoop of ice cream, chopped pecans, and more caramel on top and serve!

SOPPED-UP STAPLES,

Full of Flava

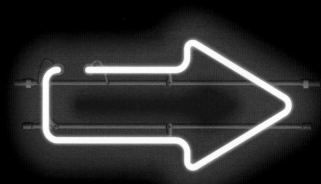

Sauces and dressings are like head turners.

They can take something from basic to all that and a bag of chips, hunny. Especially if you make something wrong, you can just throw a li'l sauce or dressing on there and it's gonna be alright. Staples are the stylists of the culinary world, dressin' things up and takin' your meal from drab to fab in no time flat. It's like adding makeup to a bare face—it's good on its own, but who doesn't love a little extra glam!

Lemme show you: That chicken breast is too dry? You just cover it up with some of my Juke Joint Ranch Dressing (page 202). If your ribs are bland, give them a good slather of my Juke Joint Whiskey BBQ Sauce (page 204). A dressing can make or break a salad, just like the right shoes with the right outfit. You could take a piece of lettuce and put a good dressing on it, and boom! It's like your food's had a good face-lift, hunny!

House SEASONING BLEND

I season my food really good to make sure it's all sopped up, and this seasoning blend will help you sop up yours! It's close to the Juke Joint Seasoning I sell on online, so you can buy it or make it yourself.

MAKES ABOUT ⅓ CUP

1 tablespoon cayenne
1 tablespoon garlic powder

1 tablespoon ground black pepper
1 tablespoon kosher salt

1 tablespoon onion powder
1 tablespoon paprika (not that smoked kind)

I. Place all the ingredients in a clean, medium jar and shake real good to mix.

2. Cover and keep in the cabinet to use as needed.

Homemade
FISH FRY

I add self-rising flour to my fish fry mix because I like the lighter texture and crunch it gives the seafood. It also keeps the fish from getting too mealy. Some folks don't like to add any flour and keep their mix all cornmeal. If you like a softer crust, you can add a little more flour to this recipe. Same goes for the spices; adjust yours to taste. Or you can always use my store-bought Juke Joint Fish Fry. There you go!

Use this mix when frying shrimp and oysters, or try it with my Southern Fried Fish (page 98) and Fried Scallops (page 107).

My mom would make a big batch and then put any extra in a heavy freezer bag in the refrigerator or freezer until ready to use. The flavors stay good and fresh that way.

MAKES A HEAPING 3 CUPS

2 cups yellow cornmeal
¼ cup garlic powder
¼ cup kosher salt
¼ cup onion powder

¼ cup self-rising flour
2 tablespoons paprika
1 tablespoon ground black pepper

1 tablespoon Accent seasoning or MSG

I. Combine all the ingredients in a big bowl and mix with your hands real good, 'cuz your hands are the best tool in the kitchen, hunny. Take a little taste from your finger after it's mixed up and adjust the seasoning to your liking.

2. Use as needed to cook your seafood.

Sopped-Up Staples, Full of Flava

Juke Joint
RANCH DRESSING

Why people eat mayonnaise by the spoonful, I don't know! Black people want a good ranch! And you're probably gonna wanna double this. I know I can't stop eatin' it once I get started.

If you want a little kick or razzle-dazzle, substitute 1 tablespoon of my store-bought Juke Joint Black Cajun Seasoning for the garlic powder, onion powder, and the salt. And be careful not to overseason your ranch; otherwise it will overpower whatever you're serving it with, which—if you're paying attention to how I'm tellin' you to cook—should already be well seasoned.

I eat this with Fried Dill Pickle Spears (page 75), Southern Fried Fish (page 98), and Fried Scallops (page 107). And I put it in my Pasta Salad (page 80).

MAKES ABOUT 2½ CUPS

1 cup buttermilk
1 cup mayonnaise (I like Duke's)
½ cup sour cream (important because it cuts that mayonnaise flava!)

2 tablespoons dried dill
2 tablespoons dried parsley
2 teaspoons garlic powder
1 teaspoon onion powder

1 teaspoon Accent seasoning or MSG (optional but really brings out the flava!)
½ teaspoon kosher salt

Combine all the ingredients in a medium bowl and whisk to combine. Adjust the seasoning to taste and serve with everything—it's that good!

Can be refrigerated for about 1 week, but it won't even last that long.

Danni's Juke Joint Comfort Food

Juke Joint
TARTAR SAUCE

This is for serving with my Southern Fried Fish (page 98) and Fried Scallops (page 107) and for those people who like dipping their French fries in tartar!

My favorite mayonnaise is Duke's: it's creamy and doesn't taste like mayo to me. All my mayo haters will understand what I'm talkin' about. I only eat mayo mixed into something.

If you feelin' frisky, add a teaspoon of Old Bay Seasoning and a few dashes (or more) of hot sauce. And if you're like my daddy, you're gonna put a whole teaspoon of black pepper, maybe mo', in yours.

MAKES ABOUT 1 CUP

½ cup mayonnaise

¼ cup sour cream

¼ cup sweet salad cubes or sweet pickle relish

2 tablespoons sugar

1 tablespoon fresh lemon juice

1 teaspoon ground black pepper, or to taste

1 teaspoon garlic powder

1 teaspoon Old Bay Seasoning (optional)

1 teaspoon onion powder

1 teaspoon kosher salt

Few dashes of hot sauce, if you like a little kick like I do

Mix all ingredients together in a medium bowl, cover, and set inside the fridge until you need it. Adjust the seasoning to taste before serving. Store, refrigerated, for up to 1 week.

Sopped-Up Staples, Full of Flava

Juke Joint
WHISKEY BBQ SAUCE

Hunny, you know I like to make a LOT of sauce when I'm making this. You can add the whiskey if you're feelin' frisky; if not, it's still good. And remember to cook this (or reheat it later) over low heat. Give it a little stir, then step back from that stove and cover it again because that simmering sauce may just pop on you. Blame science, not me!

I don't like my sauce real thick; I like it to be pourable, so I don't cook it for long. Plus that way, the whiskey doesn't cook out and you can really taste it!

This is really tasty on grilled chicken and pork chops, as well as ribs.

MAKES ABOUT 4½ CUPS

3 cups ketchup

1¼ cups packed brown sugar

½ cup apple cider vinegar

½ cup Hennessy or whatever brown liquor you like best (optional)

3 tablespoons Worcestershire sauce

2 tablespoons garlic powder

2 tablespoons liquid smoke

2 tablespoons onion powder

2 tablespoons yellow mustard

1½ teaspoons ground black pepper

Kosher salt to taste

1. Place all the ingredients in a large saucepan and stir with a fork to combine. Cover and bring to a simmer over low heat. Give it a good stir every couple minutes, cover it again, and cook until the sauce gets a dark, rich color and thickens a little, about 25 minutes. Uncover and cook for 5 more minutes.

2. Use right away, or let cool, cover tightly, and refrigerate for up to 1 month.

BUTTAS

Butta is the South's delicacy. For some people there's caviar, others love truffle salt, and they love all of those bougie and zha-zha things, but in the South, it's butter. If you don't add butter to your food, it just ain't sopped up and it ain't right. We add it to grits, pancakes, eggs, spinach, roasted veggies, desserts . . . But you'd also use butter if you burn yourself in the kitchen—it may be an old wives' remedy, but my mama would always take a little bit of butter and rub it on my wound so that I wouldn't get a blister—or for scabs and scrapes . . . So here are four delicious butters, not for burns but that you can use for a lot of the dishes throughout the book, or on anything you like. To soften your butter for mixin' it up, just let it hang out on the counter for about 2 hours or so.

Honey Butta

MAKES ½ CUP

¼ cup (½ stick) salted butter, at room temperature

½ cup honey

I. Combine the ingredients in a medium bowl and mash with a spoon until smooth.

2. Serve at room temperature or put it in a covered container or wrap in plastic wrap, refrigerate, and use whenever you want.

Cajun Juke Joint Butta

Use as a rub for chicken, fish, or vegetables, or add it to your sauces!

MAKES 1¼ CUPS

1 cup (2 sticks) salted butter, at room temperature

2 tablespoons dried parsley

1 tablespoon garlic powder

2 tablespoons onion powder

½ teaspoon ground black pepper

2 tablespoons Juke Joint Black Cajun Seasoning, or other Cajun seasoning

Combine the ingredients in a large bowl and give everything a stir until combined. Use immediately, or put it in a covered container or wrap in plastic wrap, refrigerate, and use whenever you want.

Cinnamon Crunch Butta

This is incredible! Use at your own risk on biscuits, pancakes, or toast, or mix into pies or cinnamon rolls! The best way to crush the cereal is with a food processor, but if you don't have one, you can put the cereal in a freezer bag and crush it with your hands.

MAKES ABOUT 1 CUP

½ cup (1 stick) salted butter, at room temperature

½ teaspoon ground cinnamon

¼ teaspoon kosher salt

1½ teaspoons brown sugar

½ cup crushed Cinnamon Toast Crunch cereal (you can substitute your favorite cereal; I also love using Frosted Flakes)

1. Put the butter in a medium bowl, add the cinnamon, salt, and brown sugar, and whisk together until smooth and creamy.

2. Gently fold in the crushed cereal and mix well.

3. Use immediately, or put it in a covered container or wrap in plastic wrap, refrigerate, and use whenever you want.

Garlic, Bacon & Chive Butta

This makes a meeeeeaaaan garlic bread! It's also good on French bread and hoecakes, as a rub for baked chicken, or as a topper for steak or baked potatoes. It's perfect for every savory dish. Hunny, you could spread this on a piece of charcoal and it would be sopped up!

MAKES ABOUT 1 CUP

½ cup (1 stick) salted butter, at room temperature

1 tablespoon garlic powder

½ teaspoon onion powder

½ teaspoon ground black pepper

½ cup chopped cooked bacon

¼ cup finely diced chives or scallions

1. Put the butter, garlic powder, onion powder, and black pepper in a medium bowl and whisk together until smooth and creamy.

2. Now, I want you to gently fold in those bacon bits and chives until everything is combined.

3. Use immediately, or put it in a covered container or wrap in plastic wrap, refrigerate, and use whenever you want.

♦ Cajun Juke Joint Butta

♦ Cinnamon Crunch Butta

♦ Garlic, Bacon & Chive Butta

BASIC RICE

I like jasmine rice for just about everything. It's got a great flavor. But use any long-grain rice you've got.

If you're making this rice to serve on its own, then add the salt, but do not add it if you're using this recipe as a component of the Cheesy Broccoli & Rice Casserole with Potato Chip Topping (page 159), since I've got plenty of salt in that casserole.

MAKES 3 CUPS

1 cup jasmine or other long-grain rice

1 teaspoon kosher salt (optional)

I. Combine 2 cups water, the rice, and salt (if using) in a medium pot and bring to a boil. Reduce the heat to low, cover with a tight-fitting lid, and simmer undisturbed for 15 minutes.

2. Remove from the heat and leave covered for 5 minutes to finish cooking all the way through.

SIMPLE SYRUP

This is somethin' you can whip up really quick and keep in the fridge for when you need to make yourself a good blender drink.

You can also use simple syrup to sweeten your tea or home-squeezed lemonade. This will keep for a couple months in an airtight jar in your fridge.

MAKES 1 CUP

1 cup sugar

I.   Place the sugar and 1 cup water in a small saucepan and bring to a low boil. Reduce the heat to medium low, stir, and cook until the sugar is dissolved, about 4 minutes.

2.   Cool completely before using. Transfer to an airtight container and keep refrigerated until ready to use.

UNIVERSAL CONVERSION CHART

OVEN TEMPERATURE EQUIVALENTS

250°F = 120°C

275°F = 135°C

300°F = 150°C

325°F = 160°C

350°F = 180°C

375°F = 190°C

400°F = 200°C

425°F = 220°C

450°F = 230°C

475°F = 240°C

500°F = 260°C

MEASUREMENT EQUIVALENTS

Measurements should always be level unless directed otherwise.

⅛ teaspoon = 0.5 mL

¼ teaspoon = 1 mL

½ teaspoon = 2 mL

1 teaspoon = 5 mL

1 tablespoon = 3 teaspoons = ½ fluid ounce = 15 mL

2 tablespoons = ⅛ cup = 1 fluid ounce = 30 mL

4 tablespoons = ¼ cup = 2 fluid ounces = 60 mL

5⅓ tablespoons = ⅓ cup = 3 fluid ounces = 80 mL

8 tablespoons = ½ cup = 4 fluid ounces = 120 mL

10⅔ tablespoons = ⅔ cup = 5 fluid ounces = 160 mL

12 tablespoons = ¾ cup = 6 fluid ounces = 180 mL

16 tablespoons = 1 cup = 8 fluid ounces = 240 mL

INDEX

Note: Page references in *italics* indicate photographs.

Danni Rose is a self-taught home cook, TV personality, and cookbook author who became an international Internet sensation after sharing her childhood memories and delicious yet unexpected recipes with the world. Her love for all things food, cooking, and culture began in her father's juke joint in Birmingham, Alabama, at the tender age of ten. Like Danni herself, her food is modern but packed with tons of old school flava!